Disney Never Lands

Things Disney Never Made

Jim Korkis

Theme Park Press
The Happiest Books on Earth
www.ThemeParkPress.com

Theme Park Press publishes its books in a variety of print and electronic formats. Some content that appears in one format may not appear in another.

Editor: Bob McLain
Layout: Artisanal Text

ISBN 979-8-89609-018-2
Printed in the United States of America

Theme Park Press | www.ThemeParkPress.com
Address queries to ben@themeparkpress.com

Dedicated to all the Disney Imagineers and animators who worked so hard developing some wonderful ideas that were later abandoned.

CONTENTS

Introduction

Disney has been so prolific and successful that it is hard to imagine that many of its most intriguing projects despite significant investments of time, talent and money ended up abandoned and forgotten.

Disney developed enough unfinished projects to fill several books. In fact, I wrote an entire book about one of them, the famous unmade animated feature film *Gremlins* based on the novel authored by Roald Dahl. (*Gremlin Trouble,* Theme Park Press 2017)

Projects ranging from Disney's America theme park in Virginia to the animated feature *Chanticleer* to the Dick Tracy's Crimestoppers attraction that would have been in a 1920s Chicagoland area of Disney's Hollywood Studios are missing from this book along with so many other things because of space limitations. There are more stories left to tell.

Many reasons can prevent a project from going forward including lack of sponsorship to help offset the cost, lack of existing technology to make something work, unresolved problems with the story, and not having the right talent that can make the dream a reality.

Of course a big reason is lack of money. Disney, after all, has always been a business and to remain in business must produce projects that will return more than enough money to compensate for the total cost of the project as well as a healthy profit to invest in new projects.

Imagineers and animators constantly dream up new things but most of them never get any further than some concept artwork. In some cases, perhaps a small model was prepared. Most of these dreams never materialized and it is just part of the normal development process.

Some ideas were put aside and brought back years later for another project. Walt conceived of the idea of the prince and princess dancing in the clouds for *Snow White and the Seven Dwarfs* (1937) but when he couldn't use it there, he considered it for *Cinderella* (1950). It finally appeared in *Sleeping Beauty* (1959).

Because things in this book were abandoned projects, Disney did not always maintain full documentation, artwork and definitely not models connected to them. Sometimes the only information that still exists comes from official publicity announcements or perhaps the people who worked on them and the few written souvenirs or photos they may have saved for their personal enjoyment.

When the plans for a Switzerland pavilion for Epcot's World Showcase were cancelled, the stunning concept art painting was simply tossed into a dumpster because it was no longer needed. It was saved by an Epcot executive who had it framed and hung in his office until his retirement. He generously explained details on it to me one day when I was working in his area including how it would have featured a version of Disneyland's Matterhorn.

A friend who worked as an animator on *Who Framed Roger Rabbit* (1988) showed me artwork intended for the never animated scene of the funeral of Marvin Acme. One sequence had a Fleischer Studio Superman on his knees and sobbing while holding in his hands Mighty Mouse who was also crying at the loss of their human friend who meant so much to their animation community.

As Imagineer Eddie Sotto told me when I interviewed him about several Disney projects he worked on that never got made:

> The unbuilt pavilion concepts never suffer budget cuts and always have the unfair advantage of being flawless in our imagination! There are always more ideas than there is room to put them or pay for them.

I have always been fascinated by things that were announced but never completed. I have also been equally fascinated by the stories behind those projects and why they never developed. Here are a few of my favorite stories.

—Jim Korkis
Disney Historian
May 2019

PART ONE

The Theme Parks That Never Were

As soon as Disneyland opened, hundreds of places wanted a Disneyland. Walt told writer Pete Martin that as early as 1956:

> We had them from all over. Even from all over the world. They wanted us to do one in Egypt. They wanted us to do one in Japan. They wanted us to do one in Brazil—at the capital there.

Walt famously said "you can't top pigs with pigs" to summarize his experience of releasing three other short cartoons following the extraordinary cartoon *The Three Little Pigs* (1933) that featured the same characters but never came close to matching the critical or financial success of the original.

It established Walt's belief to not repeat himself by doing the same thing but to build on what he had learned with something different which is one of the reasons when distributors wanted a series of theatrical cartoons featuring Dopey from *Snow White and the Seven Dwarfs* (1937), Walt refused even though they would have made money.

"Walt instinctively resists doing the same thing twice," said Walt's older brother Roy O. Disney to a reporter. "He likes to try something fresh."

For an interview with *LOOK* magazine in January 1964, Walt said:

> There will only be one Disneyland as such. Now that doesn't mean that in some areas we might not develop certain projects that would be compatible to that area and we are considering things of that sort.

At the 1965 press conference announcing the Florida Project, Walt said:

> We know the basic things that have family appeal. There are many ways that you can use those certain basic things and give them a new decor, a new treatment.

Imagineer Marvin Davis remembered:

> Walt always steadfastly refused to do another Disneyland because he said he had done the best park he knew how to do and why would he want to repeat himself? He said, 'There are too many things in the world to do that are different and new and more of a challenge to me.' The only reason I'm sure he decided to tackle Walt Disney World was because of its connection to Epcot.

In 1958, Walt created a brand new CircleVision 360 film for the Brussels World's Fair, *America the Beautiful.* It was then shown at the American National Exhibition in Moscow, Russia in 1959. In June of 1960 the new film debuted at Disneyland. It had been a huge success at every venue. Walt also produced the Circle Vision film *Italia '61* sponsored by Fiat for the Italia '61 Exposition in Turin.

Walt thought about building a series of CircleVision theaters around the world that would each have its own unique film that would then rotate to the other theaters.

In 1963, Walt looked at the Seagram Tower on the Canadian side of Niagara Falls as a possibility for a film focused on the area in a CircleVision theater. Also in 1963, he discussed producing a CircleVision travelogue film for St. Louis, Missouri as part of its upcoming bicentennial celebration. Walt's dream of a chain of CircleVision theaters was abandoned after his death.

The following chapters showcase the diversity of some of the entertainment venues that the Walt Disney Company has attempted over the decades.

Port Disney Long Beach (1991)

When the Disney company purchased the Wrather Corporation in 1988 to gain ownership of the Disneyland Hotel, that same package included the contracts and leases for the legendary *Queen Mary* ocean liner and Howard Hughes' *Spruce Goose* wooden airplane in Long Beach, California, as well as the Londontowne Village which was a collection of quaint shops and restaurants between the plane and the ship.

Wrather also had an option to lease about 236 acres near the *Queen Mary* that could be developed as a marina or filled in to create land that could be used for a retail district. Disney created a subsidiary company, WCO Port Properties, to oversee the Long Beach property leases.

It quickly became apparent that tourists despite all of Disney's marketing attempts were just not that interested in making the trip to Long Beach to see the two historical icons.

As Disney Marketing vice president Jack Lindquist said:

> Before [Disney] came in, the *Queen Mary* had less than a half million visitors a year and the first year we took it over, we had more than a million visitors but that was still not enough to cover the expenses for repairs and maintenance. We were losing millions of dollars each year.

The Long Beach area was certainly ripe for expansion. Even Jack Wrather before his death had huge plans for the area which is why he had an option on all of that land.

He had announced he was going to build a ten story hotel and parking garage with a large area devoted to meeting space for conventions by 1988. Then, he stated he would build a huge retail space tentatively called the Festival Marketplace followed by an exhibition hall and perhaps five to six high-rise office buildings. He passed away in 1984 before any of those plans were finalized.

Despite the tourist attractions of the *Queen Mary* and *Spruce Goose* underperforming to Disney expectations, Disney CEO Michael Eisner also saw that there was potential in the location.

At one point Eisner wanted to build a new Walt Disney Stadium for the California Angels in Long Beach as well as The Pond hockey arena for the Mighty Ducks there. In addition, he hoped the stadium might work to attract a new Los Angeles pro football team. Long Beach's lack of enthusiasm killed those proposals.

In January 1990, Eisner announced that as part of his plans for a "Disney Decade" of expansion that the Disney Company was planning on building a new theme park to be located either in Anaheim (basically on the area of the Disneyland parking lot along with some additional acreage) or in Long Beach and added, "It depends a lot on which community wants us more."

Since such an entertainment venue was guaranteed to bring in millions of dollars in tax revenue and additional jobs, Eisner was expecting major concessions from the proposed city to help facilitate its construction and make major modifications to the existing infrastructure including significant road improvements.

For Anaheim, Disney proposed WestCot, a variation of its east coast Epcot theme park. For Long Beach, the concept of a Port Disney was first presented to city and port officials in closed meetings in July 1990 and then officially announced in a public meeting on July 31, 1990.

The property would have had a nautical-themed park known as DisneySea, a marina, a cruise ship port (potentially competing with the existing Port of Los Angeles for cruise ship traffic) and an expanded specialty retail and entertainment area in addition to five resort hotels, one in the space then occupied by the Spruce Goose that would have had to be moved.

The *Queen Mary* would also need to be relocated roughly 700 feet north but would still remain as the backdrop for the new themed venue that would reportedly cost more than $2.8 billion. In October 1991, the entire project would be renamed DisneySea to avoid confusion with the Port of Long Beach.

Over the years, some have claimed that Disney never really intended to build a Port Disney in Long Beach. Supposedly, it was merely a ruse to leverage more favorable terms and concessions from the City of Anaheim for what Disney really wanted by creating a faux competition.

However, many years and millions of dollars were spent on the project and it was well known that executive Frank Wells was a huge supporter of building in Long Beach because he felt it would be less expensive than Anaheim and that there would be more space for future expansion.

In addition, many of the things developed for the Port Disney project were later included in Japan's Tokyo DisneySea theme park (that opened in 2001) so obviously the development of attractions had been taken seriously enough by the Disney company for the Oriental Land Company to decide to pursue that "seven seas" concept for their second park as early as 1992.

In fact, that park's American Waterfront area features Disney's version of the *Queen Mary* labeled the S.S. *Columbia* because some of Imagineer Tim Kirk's designs for Port Disney would have depended upon the ship as a focal point.

Actually, for quite a while, it looked like Long Beach would indeed be the final choice. However, the residents of Long Beach were not quite as beguiled by the magic of Disney as was the government of Anaheim.

Representatives from neighborhood associations and businesses objected to the significantly increased traffic concerns, the public subsidies that Disney demanded that were felt to be excessive, environmental concerns and other issues.

Surprised by this cool reception, Disney met with small groups three times a week between August 1990 and February 1991 as a community outreach and to convince them that Disney would be a good neighbor and the project important to the city.

Disney created a Port Disney project display room aboard the *Queen Mary* on the Promenade Deck in Picadilly Circus that featured a large six-by-six-foot three-dimensional model of the proposed Port Disney project and other components like concept artwork to help people better understand what Disney was planning and what it would look like.

In addition, Disney published one issue of *The Port Disney News* filled with elaborate and colorful concept art and detailed descriptions, which was mailed directly to residents of Long Beach in 1991 in the hopes of addressing any concerns and stirring up support for the project:

> Welcome to DisneySea! Here you will experience a thrilling journey through the mysteries, challenges and natural wonders of the sea. Among the highlights of your trip will be an intimate encounter with our planet's most important environmental resource and the chance to participate in exciting research activities conducted by some of the leading oceanic scientists.
>
> For millions of Southern California residents and visitors, this fantastic voyage may become a reality based on the conceptual master plan for one of the most innovative theme parks ever conceived by the Walt Disney Company.
>
> According to its designers, the goal of DisneySea is to enable everyone to experience the marvels of nature's secret world beneath the sea and to gain first-hand experience of how the oceans affect human life as well as the life of the planet.
>
> Walt Disney Imagineering, the creative, design, production and project management subsidiary of the Walt Disney Company responsible for the creation of Disney theme parks and attractions, has been charged to develop DisneySea. Its vision for

Long Beach is a singular blend of entertainment and education through Disney-style rides and attractions, marine research facilities, an oceanarium and other aquatic adventures.

While plans for DisneySea are still evolving, Walt Disney Imagineering is planning attractions for visitors to enjoy the spirit of the sea with fun as the common denominator.

The Port Disney resort complex would span roughly 414 acres on both sides of Queensway Bay. The two sides of the resort known as City-Side and Port-Side would be connected by watercraft, monorail and the Queensway Bridge.

City-Side would be the location of three Disney resort hotels, shopping and entertainment areas and would integrate existing facilities like the Hyatt Regency Hotel, the Long Beach Convention Center, Shoreline Village and the Downtown Long Beach Marina.

Disney would build three resort hotels there: the 900-room Tidelands Hotel attached to a six acre park, the 400-unit all-suite Shoreline Hotel with its own shopping center and the 700-room Marina Hotel adjacent to the Long Beach Convention Center. In addition, a new seventeen acre park would be created along with enhancements to Shoreline Drive.

Port Disney's monorail system would run alongside Shoreline Drive, and connect with these three Disney hotels before turning southwards towards the 225 acre DisneySea theme park making it one of the advantages of staying at a Disney resort hotel.

Disney would build two more resort hotels on Port-Side: the Canal Hotel with 1,400 guest rooms and 150-slip guest marina as well as a waterfront promenade and the 500-room Port Hotel with luxury accommodations and a waterfront setting. Disney later decided to downsize the Canal Hotel by about half and include an additional sixth hotel called the Regatta to keep the skyline silhouette more manageable and less overwhelming.

The WorldPort just outside the theme park on Port-Side would be the location where excursion water ferries would depart on a regular basis to Avalon, Newport Beach, Dana Point, Redondo Beach and Marina del Rey. It would have a promenade that provided easy access to shops and restaurants and would be the end of the monorail line.

It was suggested that theme boats, pageants and special events would be featured in the area where the Queen Mary would also now be docked as a familiar visual icon. In addition, at night there would be laser and fireworks shows.

For the first time, a five berth port would provide cruise ships access and also feature a 250 slip public marina. It would actually have been the largest cruise terminal on the west coast if it had been built.

In order to justify the need for 250 acres of landfill, Disney had to include marinas, a cruise ship port, ferry ports and even some sort of an aquarium in order to meet the requirements of the Coastal Commission.

One of the things that made the DisneySea theme park different than Disneyland was that it was specifically to be educationally oriented in addition to the entertainment aspects much like the original overall intent of Epcot Center in Florida or the Living Seas pavilion at Epcot. To immerse guests in this experience, a massive 17,000 space parking garage would block any unsightly view of the real world on land from the park.

Without an iconic castle, the centerpiece for the park would have been Oceana, a bubble-shaped structure with orbs reminiscent of a hidden Mickey head that housed the world's largest "oceanarium" which was a combined two story aquarium reaching depths of up to thirty feet and holding ten to twelve gallons of water and an extensive learning center.

In fact, Oceana would house the Future Research Center that was to be a working meeting center for oceanographic researchers as well as the Ocean Outreach Center described as a "library of the sea". It would have been a massive research library dedicated to all aspects of the ocean throughout the world with computers, reading rooms, research files, and full access to ocean-centric literature for everyone from guests to scientists.

It was hoped that respected scientists from around the world would visit to conduct studies because of the vastness of the available resources.

For the average guest there would be interactive exhibits to learn about the ocean and marine life, a submarine simulator going to various underwater locations and even an exhibit to demonstrate how to clean up an oil spill.

Overhead walkways and underwater portholes would provide views of the marine creatures. Kids would be able to borrow goggles that allowed them to appreciate what it was like to see as a fish.

Project Manager David Malmuth said, "Our goal is to sensitize millions of visitors each year to the enormous challenges and opportunities of our seas—our most precious resource—in a setting that encourages play and fantasy."

Oceana would truly be the centerpiece as all the other themed places would surround it much like ripples around a pebble dropped into a body of water.

According to the *Port Disney News:*

> Guests will be able to visit the heart of this functioning sea laboratory, observing scientists at work. Watching these experts, vis-

itors can glimpse the future of man's involvement with the seas and probe deeper into man's relationship with the environment. For the more light-hearted adventurers, the Center will include a simulator adventure that will give guests a glimpse of the drama—and danger—faced by real explorers of the deep.

Just as Disneyland had several different lands, there were several different sections of DisneySea:

Mysterious Island

The icon was a man-made volcano and the area centered around stories of Captain Nemo and his *Nautilus* submarine. It featured several attractions including a ride discovering the lost City of Atlantis, Pirate Island (described as "Tom Sawyer's Island times 10"), and Nemo's Lava Cruiser (where suspended guests would careen through underground caverns in the volcano).

Heroes' Harbor

This area was themed as an ancient Greek village where "the myths and legends of the sea come to life". It featured attractions like the Aqua-Labyrinth that was a "challenging maze with walls made only of water", a ride that was to based on the voyages of Sinbad the Sailor and another attraction centering on the adventures of Ulysses from Homer's famous poem.

Fleets of Fantasy

Near the boardwalk area, it was described by Disney as "a harbor of fabled and fanciful ships, including outsized Chinese junks and Egyptian galleys, would disguise exciting rides and dining and entertainment experiences."

Venture Reefs

This area originally known as "Adventure Reefs" seemed reminiscent of Florida's Typhoon Lagoon water park. Guests had the opportunity to surf or snorkel through tropical reefs filled with fish or just enjoy the paradise-like setting and swim. One piece of art shows guests being lowered in a steel cage into a tank of sharks.

The *Port Disney News* stated:

> Guests will enjoy scenic beach vistas from the Caribbean, Polynesian, and the Pacific. They'll be entertained and invited to dine, shop, and take a dip in the ocean, where they'll find sunken ships and marine life "under the sea."

Boardwalk and Rainbow Pier

Designed as a tribute to Long Beach's famous Pike amusement park, this area would include a Ferris wheel and an old-fashioned wooden roller coaster.

Such a massive undertaking could not be done all at once so Disney announced that like Walt Disney World, the park would open in two phases. The first phase would be operating by the year 2000 with the second and final phase completed by 2010. The expectation was that the first year would attract up to ten million guests and Disney anticipated that it would be a minimum eighteen hour experience to enjoy most of the area.

Disney officially cancelled the project in December 1991 and announced it would instead proceed with the Anaheim WestCot proposal. Many things ended up killing the Port Disney project.

A special bill would have needed to be passed by California to permit Disney to proceed with the landfill and allow recreational use of the new property. The bill stalled in the California State Senate and was actively opposed by the Sierra Club and the California Coastal Commission fearing it would set a bad precedent. Disney was preceived as being "arrogant" in how they proposed the bill.

Disney would have had to also restore wetlands elsewhere at a significant cost to mitigate the marine environmental impact and couldn't come to an agreement on the amount of land to be restored. Significant financial overruns for the EuroDisneyland project in France drained working capital forcing not only the abandonment of this project but also eventually WestCot in Anaheim.

The City of Long Beach was greatly divided about the project as well as the money it would need to contribute to do things like improvements to the Long Beach Freeway and other roads because of all the additional traffic. Internal disputes kept delaying action and preventing commitments from being formalized. Basically, local, state, and federal approvals were all required instead of just the Anaheim City Council.

Long Beach Mayor Ernie Kell told the *Los Angeles Times* on December 13, 1991, "Obviously, we're very disappointed. I had hoped we would be able to work this out."

"I can't believe the lack of leadership and vision that cost us this quality corporation," lamented Long Beach Councilman Jeffrey A. Kellogg and blamed both the harbor commissioners and the mayor for not finding a way to keep Disney.

Councilman Evan Anderson Braude said he saw no reason why "an agreement could not have been reached. Highly questionable negotiation tactics (by the port) were apparently employed, and they appear to have backfired."

WestCot (1991)

In 1987, Disney executives, including Jack Lindquist, began seriously talking about a second gated theme park in Anaheim based on already existing elements from Florida's Epcot to create a west coast version to be called WestCot or WestCot Center to reference Epcot's original name.

Lindquist had been advocating for a second Disney park in Anaheim as early as 1982 but continually met with resistance.

The cost of the project was estimated at $3.1 billion dollars with construction beginning in 1992 and an opening date of 1998. The hope was to make the Disneyland area a multiple-night vacation destination stay, like Walt Disney World, and to attract 25 million visitors a year. WestCot alone was projected to bring in at least ten million guests just in the first year.

Lindquist mentioned an area north of the park with those offices moving to a new building Disney had purchased from Global Van Lines. He also mentioned the famous 40-acre strawberry farm across West Street. Lindquist assured the audience that the parking lot area was no longer a consideration. However, that was exactly the area finally chosen with the addition of some other surrounding acreage Disney owned.

The Master Plan for WestCot with a proposed budget was released to the public on May 8, 1991, but was already being downsized by 1992 (with the removal of things like a Hollywoodland section in the New World area), and by 1995, the project was completely dead.

Many factors were involved including costing too much money, Anaheim not wanting to pay for some things and make some other concessions, the possible need to relocate some Anaheim residents, community discontent about things like light pollution, Disney wanting its own special assessment district like Reedy Creek in Florida and the failure of EuroDisneyland draining financial resources from the Disney Company among other factors.

CEO Michael Eisner announced that as part of the "Disney Decade" of the 1990s, Disney would build another theme park in Southern California. The company also explored the possibility of a nautically-themed park called Port Disney in Long Beach where it was operating the Queen Mary and the Spruce Goose.

At the same time, he proposed the WestCot project for Anaheim. With typical Eisner tact, he told the public:"It depends a lot on which community wants us more."

Since such an entertainment venue was guaranteed to bring in millions of dollars in tax revenue and additional jobs, Eisner was expecting major concessions from whichever proposed city was chosen to help facilitate its construction and for them to make major modifications to the existing infrastructure including road improvements because of the expected increased traffic.

Eventually, Disney found too many challenges with the Long Beach project and so in December 1991 officially announced it was abandoning it and would be proceeding with WestCot in Anaheim.

While inspired by Epcot and its core philosophy of technological innovaton and international culture and borrowing some of its attractions, WestCot would be different because of signiciant space limitations and the urban setting surrounding the park.

WestCot would have been divided into two sections: Ventureport (the hub for this version of Epcot's Futureworld) and World Showcase similar in tone to Epcot's version but very different with only four pavilions representing a larger range of international cultures.

The entrance to WestCot featured a 300-foot golden sphere called SpaceStation Earth on a lush green island and featured a new omnimover attraction inside called Cosmic Journeys. The silver Spaceship Earth on the other side of the country was a mere 180 feet high.

To reach the sphere required crossing over a bridge and walking under a cascading waterfall, to enter a huge lobby where guests could then ride the attraction or proceed to the three Ventureport pavilions. Just beyond this icon would be Ventureport, "a futuristic gateway from which guests embark on magical journeys to the Wonders of WestCot themed pavilions."

The pavilions included the Wonders of Living, Wonders of Earth, and Wonders of Space. They would all be enclosed so that Disney could control the entire experience.

Imagineer Tony Baxter said:

> We hope that when you come away from those experiences you will have less fear and apprehension about becoming a part of that world.

Surrounding the perimeter would be the four additional pavilions in the World Showcase not representing individual countries but geographical regions known here as the Four Corners of the World: Asia, Europe, the Americas, and Africa.

The pavilions were called "The Seven Wonders of WestCot."

The Wonders of Earth pavilion would allow guests to be immersed in exotic environments, such as a jungle, the desert, underwater, or the frozen world of the Arctic. It would also include an attraction based on Charles and Ray Eames' *Powers of Ten* film.

The Wonders of Living pavilion would be focused on the human mind and body and feature the Epcot attractions Body Wars, Cranium Command, The Making of Me, and a different version of the Journey Into Imagination attraction but still featuring Dreamfinder and Figment.

The Wonders of Space pavilion would feature "a journey through the Cosmos" based on work that had been done on a proposed but never built Space Pavilion for Epcot.

The Four Corners of the World would have had the New World (the Americas) with a United States turn-of-the-century Main Street, an updated version of Epcot's the American Adventure attraction, a Native American spirit lodge show (Canada), and a Mexican fiesta show and restaurant along with another spirit show reflecting the Inca and Aztec cultures.

The Old World (Europe) would have the Circlevision 360 film *Timekeeper*, a Greek amphitheater, a Tivoli Gardens playground for children, and a James Bond-style chase aboard the Trans-European Express railroad featuring famous European buildings zooming past outside the windows.

The World of Asia would have the thrill ride called Ride the Dragon, a roller coaster that followed along the Great Wall of China into the Dragon's Teeth Mountain. The trains would be designed to look like the ever-twisting Chinese Lion-Dragon that is often seen in parades.

At its peak, guests would have been prevented from seeing outside the park by billowing red and gold silks that engulfed the moving cars. Architectural details from Japan, China, and India would be blended together in this land.

For smaller children there would have been a carousel but instead of horses, it would be composed of mythical Asian animals from all the cultures represented in the area. A white marble Indian palace would have housed a dining and entertainment area.

Also proposed for this area were a copy of Tokyo Disneyland's Meet the World show, a Three Great Religions of the World show (that was soon eliminated because of possible controversy) and a Story Teller Tree show.

The World of Africa included a white water raft ride down the fictional Congobezi River, African drummers performing outside, a farming culture exhibit, and plans when the park expanded to include an Egyptian palace.

The World Showcase area would have been home to the World Cruise also known as "The River of Time," which would have been the longest Disney ride ever at forty-five minutes. There were five ports of call roughly nine minutes apart from each other. In some ways, it was similar in concept to the Disneyland Railroad serving not just as transportation but to give an overview of the area.

During the cruise around the World Showcase there were scenes under each pavilion depicting audio animatronics recreations of moments like Leonardo da Vinci working on the Mona Lisa, the burning of Rome, and Michelangelo painting the Sistine Chapel among other key tableaus much like the ones in Epcot's Spaceship Earth.

The scenes would tell the story of the cultures of each pavilion and the evolution of world civilization. Each of the five stations would support the scenes just witnessed.

The buildings of World Showcase would have been built as six-story structures with the first three floors housing attractions, retail shops, shows, and restaurants but with the top three floors featuring hotel guest rooms. It would be the first Disney hotel within one of its theme parks and the program was called "The Live the Dream Program".

From the *Los Angeles Times* May 9, 1991:

> Also proposed for the 470-acre Disneyland Resort are three new hotels, a seven-acre public plaza and a collection of retail, dining and entertainment facilities called Disneyland Center to be built around a six-acre lake.

The Public Esplanade between Disneyland and WestCot would feature the Disneyland Center (shopping, dining, entertainment, much like the later Downtown Disney and with fountains and extensive landscaping), the Disneyland Bowl (a 5,000 seat live entertainment amphitheater, much like the Universal Amphitheater and would be located between the main plaza and the Harbor Boulevard entrance to the park), and the Disneyland Plaza (transportation hub).

There would be three huge parking structures around the perimeter of the resort (one on the northwest side near Ball Road and a pair of others on the east side near the Melodyland Church) that featured moving sidewalks that would go to a PeopleMover system that would shuttle up to 8,000 tourists an hour from the parking structures to the parks and hotels. Disney wanted new off-ramps from the Interstate 5 freeway that would directly feed into the project's parking structures and expected Anaheim to foot that bill.

The Disneyland Hotel would undergo an extensive renovation and expansion, as well with the addition of a 300 room tower. There would also be the upscale and pricey New Disneyland Resort Hotel, inspired by the Hotel Del Coronado in San Diego, with only 800 rooms. The 1,800-room WestCot Lake Resort would wrap around a six-acre lake with shops and restaurants. Pedestrian bridges would connect the hotel to a monorail station at the water's edge.

Roughly, WestCot itself would use up to 100 acres and more than 100 acres would be needed for hotels and dozens of acres reserved for parking.

Before the official announcement, Disney quietly began acquiring additional tracts of land on the perimeter of Disneyland, primarily purchasing several low-rise motels at an estimated cost of ten of thousands of dollars per room.

Disney also planned on renaming West Street between Katella Avenue and Ball Road as Disneyland Drive transforming it into a gently curving, tree-lined boulevard and home to the three new hotels.

Bruce E. Thorp, a Philadelphia-based Disney analyst with Provident National Bank, told the *Los Angeles Times*:

> [The Epcot theme has] shown itself to have tremendous lasting power that lends itself to the development in Southern California. There is nothing in their plans that disappoints me or surprises me. I would be more concerned if Disney went off on a tangent they had not done before. This addition could keep visitors on Disney property for up to a week.

At the 1994 NFFC convention, Imagineer Tony Baxter talked about how WestCot would have been a different Disney park experience. First, it was designed to be a more participatory and immersive environment so that the guests truly became part of the story Disney was attempting to tell. Second, it would be the first Disney park where guests could spend the night inside the park.

When WestCot was cancelled, CEO Michael Eisner held a three-day executive retreat in Aspen, Colorado to come up with a new idea to use that area. At that meeting of about thirty executives devised the idea for a California-based themed park that became Disney's California Adventure, which opened in 2001 on the same property that would have featured WestCot.

St. Louis Riverfront Square (1964)

In December 2015, the only known existing copy of the blueprints for Walt Disney's Riverfront Square project in St. Louis, Missouri sold for $27,000, after the auction house predicted a final price of somewhere between $5,000-$7,000. Those plans are now in the hands of a private collector and unavailable to researchers.

Walt Disney grew up in Missouri in the cities of Marceline and Kansas City. Even though he was born in Chicago, Illinois, he considered Missouri his home.

In 1945, he wrote:

> I feel that my roots are in the great state of Missouri and that I am a Missourian in every sense of the word, even to the "Show Me" tradition. Missouri typifies good, common sense Americanism, whether your roots are in the farm or in the streets of its bustling cities. I guess you can gather from this that I still have a fine warm spot for the old home state.

The city of St. Louis had been founded in 1764 and in the early 1960s plans were made to celebrate its upcoming bicentennial with the building of the Gateway Arch (opened October 1965) and the multipurpose Busch Memorial Stadium (opened May 1966).

Part of the planning for the stadium included setting aside some land just a few blocks to the north to be called Riverfront Square, an outdoor mall about 300-feet long, that would be developed with theaters, restaurants, and stores with all automobile traffic excluded.

One of the theaters would have been in the shape of a steamboat and be called the Gilded Cage and show old silent movies during the day and some evenings would host live melodrama performances. The entire mall facing the Mississippi River would have featured 19th century architecture glorifying the age when St. Louis was a popular river port.

In 1963, business and civic leaders approached Walt with the proposal that he produce a film to honor the city's history as part of the celebration as well as being part travelogue of the city as it was today. The intention was to build a 1,000-seat modified Circle Vision theater where Walt's 15-minute film would run continuously. At that point, Walt had produced other Circle Vision films that had been shown throughout the world and was interested in doing more.

Although he considered the proposal for a few weeks, Walt wasn't as enthused about the idea as he was intrigued by the land that had been set aside especially since he had become deeply interested in city planning at the time. He talked with Raymond Witcoof, president of Downtown St. Louis Inc., a group of businessmen who were involved with the downtown development.

The CCRC (Civic Center Redevelopment Corporation) invited Walt to be a consultant on the project. Walt and his brother Roy met with some of members at the Disney Studio in Burbank on March 28, 1963.

After the meeting, Walt immediately assigned Harrison "Buzz" Price and his Economics Research Associates to explore the St. Louis project and how many potential visitors might come to see the Arch and the stadium and how much money they might spend and create a feasibility study.

Price was the one who had been involved in helping select the land for Disneyland and later Walt Disney World, and was the person Walt always went to when he was considering a new project involving the purchase of land.

Walt and his wife Lillian personally visited the city along with their daughter Sharon and her husband Robert on May 20 to tour the area and see the ongoing construction on the Arch. It was assumed that Walt was just checking to see if the Disney Company might participate in some way with the celebration.

Walt and his staff were deeply involved with their commitments of creating four pavilions for the 1964-65 New York World's Fair so were hesitant to make any immediate decision on St. Louis and any possible level of participation.

Price's report in August showed that the St. Louis project could be modestly profitable with enough visitors from both the local population, as well as ones coming from out of town to see the Arch and events at the stadium to quickly recover the initial investment.

It turned out that Walt was interested in doing the entire venue. He felt that if the Disney name was going to be connected in any way that Disney had to be responsible for the entire thing to make sure it kept to his philosophies and standards. On November 18 at a press conference, he outlined his vision for Riverfront Square if it were built and operated by the Disney Company.

The central theme would be the history of St. Louis as well as the lore of the Mississippi River and the Old West. He actually said that there were things that he was envisioning that would "make parts of Disneyland obsolete." The venue would be entertaining but also educational and respectful.

He stated at the press conference:

Missouri and the history of Missouri are important to me. I was raised on a farm not far from Hannibal. There's a lot of opportunity to do things exciting about the state, the Mississippi River, Mark Twain...things both entertaining and educational. I am not interested in a tourist trap attraction. I want something we can be proud of and St. Louis can be proud of.

While he did not make a definite commitment at the time, people were excited. They were very excited until he also announced that liquor would not be served anywhere in the complex. Just like at Disneyland, it was Walt's feelings that in a family venue, alcohol had the tendency to change the tone and encourage "rowdies".

After the press conference, Anheuser-Busch beer baron August Busch Jr., a very powerful man in St. Louis and the state, supposedly made the remark that "any man who would build something like this and then not serve beer and liquor is crazy!"

According to Disney mythology that statement resulted in Walt abandoning the project on the spot and then finding another location in central Florida.

It is a myth. Walt kept planning for many months after the incident. Busch may also have been upset because in the original plans for the Riverfront Square there would have been a themed bar and restaurants, all proudly serving his product especially since he was part of the development committee. He was also planning on building a museum near Riverfront Square to honor his company's heritage and offer some free beer samples.

Preston Estep, the chairman of the CCRC, declared:

> Any plans developed by either Mr. Disney or anyone else would not be approved if they did not make provision for the sale of beer, wine and liquor in the restaurants and other appropriate entertainment facilities in the area.

A local newspaper also agreed:

> Can't Mr. Disney who wants to incorporate Missouri history and Missouri flavor into the project realize on his part that a Sahara in downtown St. Louis would be somewhat out of character?

That same November was when Walt and his staff headed south to Florida in a plane and determined that the swamps of central Florida would be the future home of the Florida Project.

Shockingly, Walt felt that Florida was not an alternative to St. Louis, but that he and his staff could build both venues at the same time. It was never a case that when the St. Louis project collapsed, Walt started looking around for an alternative location although some of the things planned for St. Louis were later incorporated into the Magic Kingdom.

The following year on March 16, 1964, Walt had another press conference after several more meetings with the CCRC officials. He had refined his ideas into a single, five-story (one story or more would be underground since they could dig down at least 112 feet), enclosed building covering two city blocks.

It was enclosed so that it could operate year round despite the weather. One of Walt's concerns was the cost to heat and cool the interior of such a structure year round and he had research done on that issue to determine that it was feasible.

In terms of the sale of alcoholic beverages, Walt had developed a compromise that it would be limited to areas restricted to adults only. Walt proposed an observation floor with picture windows overlooking the Arch and could be entered directly by special elevators, avoiding the amusement areas.

The floor would contain a formal restaurant, banquet space and a 150-seat cocktail lounge. All those areas would sell beer, wine and alcohol, but would be restricted to adults. Those adults who wanted to visit the amusement area would have a special hand stamp and not be allowed to carry beverages into the area.

This compromise was agreed to by Busch and the others and Walt still had his barrier between the alcohol and the entertainment.

Walt had Imagineer Marvin Davis design the plans just as he had for Disneyland and later for Walt Disney World. He had finished the plans by February 1964.

Thirteen pages of blueprints were produced. Conservatively, the cost for the project was $40 million, with expectations of at least 25,000 guests per day.

The plans for the interior of the indoor theme park were fluid and the specifics were never exactly addressed. As far as Walt was concerned, planning had just begun so there was no need to tie things down permanently yet, especially without the reaction of the CCRC or a definite budget.

The general concept was that half of the 600 foot, three and a half acre building would represent St. Louis at the turn of the century (early 1900s) and the other half New Orleans before the Civil War (approximately 1850).

Lighting would be used to create a cloud-filled sky on the high ceiling and speakers would pipe in vintage sound effects, like the sound of horses clip clopping on a street and appropriate music.

A Bayou Boat Ride would take guests through a Louisiana swamp and down a waterfall into the lower basement 60-foot high, and then back up a waterfall at the end. It didn't feature pirates but did include alligators and other wildlife.

Those historical scoundrels were reserved for the "Jean Lafitte Adventure Ride," where the famous pirate would be joined by other scallywags from New Orleans in an attraction similar to the original walk through attraction planned for Disneyland where guests could tour a pirate ship. Later plans included them in the Bayou Boat Ride.

A "Haunted House" would have included a stretching room to take guests to a lower floor for a "room of illusions," but some of the ghosts would be themed to actual Missouri ghost tales.

Besides a haunted house and a pirates' attraction, the French Quarter would include restaurants (including a full-sized steamboat in an indoor lake), shops and even a live show. The area would be surrounded by a diorama of the city during the time period with an emphasis on it being a port for the Mississippi River.

The St. Louis section would include a Circle Vision theater that featured a 15-minute film that showed a trip down the Mississippi River perhaps ending with a helicopter trip through the Arch.

Walt also was thinking of a theater with a 200-degree screen and interactive elements to tell the history of St. Louis. Again, the actual content of this film experience was never completely settled. It might have included the stories and characters of Mark Twain to illustrate the 1800s or may have focused on a collection of historic milestones like Lindbergh's flight or the 1904 St. Louis World's Fair.

Walt also had plans for the Old Opera House to feature a live-action show inspired by the Golden Horseshoe Revue in Disneyland, but themed to St. Louis and specifically including French can-can dancers.

There were plans for Fantasyland dark rides, like at Disneyland, and the placeholders on the blueprints were Peter Pan Flight (the most popular of the Disneyland dark rides) and either Snow White Adventures or a new attraction based on Pinocchio.

Basically, Walt was not sure he wanted to include the Disney characters, because it would distract from the illusion he wanted to create by focusing on local culture and regional history.

Walt preferred that the dark rides somehow be tied to the history of St. Louis and the Mississippi River. One suggestion was a gentle roller coaster thrill ride through Mississippi River caves while another was a more leisurely Native American canoe ride. At one point, there was talk to utilize the legends of Davy Crockett and Mike Fink as the basis for the water ride.

A proposal for an attraction based on the great St. Louis fire of 1849 was rejected because New York's Freedomland had a similar attraction based on a Chicago fire. Walt rejected a ride based on the famous Missouri outlaws Frank and Jesse James because he did not want to glorify criminals. It was the same reason he had rejected doing a Frontierland show about them for his weekly television show.

It was considered to bring in the Great Moments with Mr. Lincoln attraction from the New York World's Fair because it would only cost for transportation and installation and save expenses.

Imagineers suggested other possible Audio-Animatronics figures more closely aligned with Missouri, including Thomas Jefferson and Napoleon discussing the Louisiana Purchase, Will Rogers, John Philip Sousa, Charles Lindbergh and his *Spirit of St. Louis* plane, President Teddy Roosevelt, and local sports heroes from the turn of the century—although none were specifically identified.

It was suggested that it be presented in a theater with multiple revolving stages featuring several figures and sets much in the style of the later Country Bear Jamboree theater.

Many suggestions came and went, including a Lewis and Clark Adventure Ride that would take guests on a boat tour through dioramas and audio-animatronics figures representing people they encountered on their journey. A Merrimac Cave ride, an Old Water Wheel, a tribute to John Audubon in an aviary exhibit with live birds and more were some of the many ideas tossed around.

Always looking to the future, as he was working on this project, Walt considered other future small Disney parks, including one in Kansas City tied in with Hallmark Company's founder Joyce Hall's plans for an elaborate park, mall and zoo.

What caused the project that was so close to being built to fall apart was not a dispute over alcohol but of money and what St. Louis was willing to do for and with Disney. It was the same situation that existed in Florida, but got resolved when the Florida Governor and the state pledged 100% cooperation to make the dream a reality. Perhaps they had seen what had happened in St. Louis.

The Disney Company's understanding was that they would be responsible for all the costs related to the "show," meaning the design and building of the rides, creating the films, attention to theming, training the staff, etc.

They felt that St. Louis would provide the massive building, building parking garages, land improvement (including street traffic) and selling the land itself at a bargain price like they were getting in Florida. St. Louis would later be reimbursed from the net profits of the operation resulting in Disney eventually owning the entire development.

St. Louis was required not to build just the shell of the building, but to deliver a facility ready for the installation of the shows and attractions with all the walls and infrastructure. St. Louis felt it should only be responsible for the basic shell with Disney responsible for anything in the interior.

In July 1965, the city and Disney jointly announced that the project would not proceed. In a joint statement from the CCRC officials and Disney, it stated:

> We were asked to try to develop a major attraction having the impact on the St. Louis area of a Disneyland. We suggested at the outset that a project of that scope, in size and cost, might well prove difficult to accomplish, due to a number of imponderable factors. Such has proved to be the case.

In November 1965, Disney officially announced its plans to build an entertainment venue in central Florida. It is hard to believe that Walt felt he could build both projects concurrently, but the cancellation of the St. Louis project allowed for more attention to be paid to Walt Disney World.

The Marceline Project: Walt's Boyhood Farm (1957)

Walt Disney wrtoe in the September 23, 1938, Golden Jubilee edition of the *Marceline News*:

> Everything connected with Marceline [Missouri] was a thrill to us [the Disney family], coming, as we did, from a city the size of Chicago. The cows, pigs, and chickens gave me a big thrill, and, perhaps, that's the reason we use so many barnyard animals in the Mickey Mouse and Silly Symphony pictures today.

> Who knows? You know what the psychologists say about the importance of childhood impressions.

Walt's daughter Diane told me:

> He spoke with such warmth and joy [about Marceline]. It wasn't until I was older that I realized that he had only lived there about five years. I really thought he had spent his whole life there in Marceline.

In 1950, when designing a barn for the backyard workshop of his home in Holmby Hills, California, Walt designed it as an exact replica of the one on his family farm in Marceline.

Walt had a sincere and passionate commitment to wildlife and nature. It was an awareness that was born from his early childhood years on his family's farm in Marceline and remained with him for the rest of his life. He wanted to share that awareness with modern generations of children who would never have that same opportunity since the world was changing so quickly.

That desire was the inspiration for a personal entertainment non-profit venue project that was called The Marceline Project and later Walt's Boyhood Farm. It was abandoned after Walt's passing and the need to commit all resources to the Florida Project later called Walt Disney World.

Marceline is about 120 miles northeast of Kansas City and was incorporated on March 6, 1888. The Atchison, Topeka and Santa Fe Railway built a line from Chicago and Kansas City in 1887, and Marceline was developed along the route as a stop for refueling, water and crew changes. The train no longer stops there and hasn't for quite a few decades.

In the spring of 1906, Flora and Elias Disney were living in Chicago, Illinois with their five children: Herbert, 17; Raymond, 15; Roy, 12; Walt, 4; and 2-year-old Ruth. Chicago was rapidly growing and as part of that growth, the violent crime rate was also increasing and this worried Elias.

Elias' brother Robert already owned a 500-acre farm in Marceline, and so Elias decided that Marceline would be a good place to raise his family in a healthier environment. Elias purchased a one-story house and 45 acres of land just north of the city limits for $125 an acre.

Walt had fond memories of his childhood in Marceline, in later years often corresponded with people still in the town, and always made time for visitors from Marceline no matter how busy he was if they happened to drop by the Disney Studios.

Walt spent roughly five formative years in Marceline from 1906-1911 and its influence on him is easily seen in aspects of Disney films and Disneyland.

With the popularity of Walt's weekly television program and the opening of Disneyland, Walt was quite well-known so it was no surprise that Marceline decided to honor its favorite son. The city fathers wrote to the Disney Studios asking if they could have permission to name their new swimming pool and park after Walt.

At first, the Disney Studio was suspicious that the Marceline city fathers were looking for a sizable financial contribution, but once they were assured that everything had already been paid for (about $78,500), they agreed. Walt wrote back that he was thrilled and inquired whether there was to be an official dedication that he could attend.

The Walt Disney Municipal Park and Swimming Pool was to be dedicated July 4, 1956 in Marceline. Posters and banners welcomed back the two Disney brothers who arrived the day before the event. At the time, the population of the town was 3,172. Today the population is closer to 2,500.

Festivities during Walt and Roy's visit included Walt judging a local bathing beauty contest and the premiere of a new Disney live action film, *The Great Locomotive Chase* at the Marceline Uptown Theater.

Kaye Malins, who attended the premiere as a child, recalled:

> Walt and Roy stood outside and greeted every child that went into the theater. When Walt took the stage that day he said, "You children are lucky to live in Marceline. My best memories are the years I spent here."

Walt and Roy took time to leisurely meet with the townspeople and explore their old haunts from the local school to a huge tree that had been on the Disney farm.

During his time in Marceline for the dedication, Walt reveled in memories of his boyhood there.

After the official dedication of the park and pool, there was a small display of fireworks in the sky.

Event organizers had avoided giving the Disney families rooms in Marceline's Hotel Allen because it lacked air conditioning but they didn't want the families to stay in a hotel in nearby Brookfield.

Rush and Inez Johnson had a brand new house on 905 North Kansas Avenue and the Disneys stayed there while the Johnson family stayed with neighbors.

Walt and Lillian slept in the room of the Johnsons' seven-year-old daughter Kaye. The Johnson home was one of only three locations in Marceline that had central air conditioning in 1956. They had helped a friend who was getting into the air-conditioning business and wanted to try out his new product on their house.

Inez Johnson remembered:

> I reminded my husband that we had spent my furniture money on the air conditioning. We thought, "We can't have the Disneys on the hand-me-down furniture."

> Of course, everyone in town knew the Disneys were coming. In those days, we didn't have social media, but word got around. Our friends had very nice furniture, but no air conditioning, so they said, "We'll help you." And they furnished our house with their good stuff.

> Then they hired the chef of the Santa Fe Railroad driving car to cook for the Disneys while they were here. What an impression he made with that chef's hat. As it turned out all that fussing was for nothing, they were the dearest, warmest people and didn't care for any fanciness.

Rush Johnson recalled:

> After everything was over, he and I retired to our den. He settled back in an easy chair and sipped some scotch as he talked about his memories of his hometown.

> He said he had a dream to re-create that time, have a turn-of-the-century farm that people could visit with pigs, chickens, horses, cows, a swimming hole, field of grain, orchards and so much more.

> He asked, "Rush, who owns the Disney family farm?" I told him and he said, "You can buy it cheaper than I can. Buy it."

Johnson's daughter, Kaye Malins, said:

> He was such a visionary. He said there will come a time when a child will not know what an acre of land is. There will come

a time when a child will not know what happens when you put a seed in the ground. We're there now.

When Rush expressed concern that Marceline was too off the beaten track to support such a project, Walt smiled and told him that to just wait until during introductions to the popular weekly Disney television program Walt would look at the camera and smile and say, "When you are visiting Missouri, make sure you stop by and see my boyhood farm" and just like Disneyland, there would be shows devoted to the building and continuing operation of the attraction.

For security purposes, it was called the Marceline Project with no reference to Disney for fear that the cost of the necessary land would soar if people knew Disney was building something.

Actually Walt had written a letter a decade earlier in 1946 to Floyd Shoemaker, then the executive director of the State Historical Society of Mississippi at the University of Missouri-Columbia exploring a similar idea.

Johnson, Bill Washam and others from Marceline formed a board of directors for a not-for-profit educational foundation. Harrison "Buzz" Price and his ERA company had done a preliminary survey for Walt that showed even with all the publicity Walt could give to the venue, it would still be difficult to turn a reasonable profit. So, Walt decided it would a non-profit venture.

Rush first bought the forty-five acres that comprised the Disney house and original farm acreage. Then Walt requested that adjacent farmland should also be purchased for expansion.

Rush Johnson recalled:

> Walt expected Marcelians to come up with funding that he would match from his private corporation, Retlaw Enterprises. FHA was willing to commit one to two million dollars which excited Walt but when FHA mentioned going as high as six million dollars, Walt said we would have to go to Roy for matching funds on that amount.
>
> Roy was excited about the project but not as excited as Walt. Roy would remind me that his brother was a dreamer and not always realistic. Roy would actually spend more time asking me about his old classmates, especially the girls.
>
> We made many phone calls back and forth and over the decade I made about ten or twelve trips out to the studio. Over that time I became not only a business partner but a friend.
>
> He always had a map of Marceline on his desk in the upper left corner and his secretary told me it was always there, not just pulled out for my visit. When I visited, we would go over it in detail.

Almost immediately, he had sketched out roughly in pencil on a sheet of paper his plans of what he wanted the place to be.

Among other things, he had sketched in a motel in the upper right of the property for people to stay. In the middle left was the fishing lake. Nearby was a barn for a barn dance activity and a café.

Activities for children would include what he wrote as a "buggy train, miniature golf and a horseshoes area." In addition he had plans to re-create an old-time butcher shop, barbershop, general store, haberdashery, pool hall, and an old service station.

Inez Johnson stated:

> His rural influence as a young boy stayed with Walt for his entire life. He knew that the simple pleasures of life are worth more than we sometimes think they are. Walt imagined a living history farm where young and old could relive a simpler time and discover the roots of this country.

Rush and attorney Harry Porter worked with the Missouri Highway Commission to encourage it to build a three mile stretch of four lane road north from Marceline to U.S. 36 the heavily traveled road connecting Hannibal on the east and St. Joseph on the west. The Commission was planning to buy more right-of-way for the expansion and was doing surveys.

Then Governor Warren Hearnes who had been let in on the plans but sworn to confidentially helped persuade the highway commission to approve the road expansion. The Missouri Division of Resources (tourism) and the Missouri Division of Commerce Industrial Development became involved as well.

When changes were being made at Disneyland, Walt donated the Disneyland Midget Autopia attraction to Marceline in 1966 and the official dedication was scheduled for July fourth. With the help of Admiral Joe Fowler overseeing the installation and training, it ran for eleven years. It remains the only Disney ride ever to be relocated and operated.

Days before the ceremony, Walt cancelled attending, saying that he had a cough he just couldn't shake. A few months later in December, he would pass away from lung cancer.

With Walt's death in 1966, work on the project slowed considerably as all the resources of the Walt Disney Company were focused on the building of Walt Disney World. With Roy's death in 1971, the project was completely abandoned.

Retlaw Enterprises had purchased roughly 250–300 acres with options on up to 500 more acres. Those were then resold to the Walt Disney Company.

Time, talent and money could not be used on a project that wouldn't generate immediate needed income for the company. With Roy's death in 1971, the project was completely abandoned and Rush helped sell off the land at half what the Walt Disney Company had paid for it.

While selling off the land holdings, Rush bought the original Disney 45 acres that included the Disney family house, the Dreaming Tree and more.

The current owner, Kaye Malins, raised her family there. When she married Wally Malins, her parents gave the couple the Disney family home and farm as a wedding present. Today Kaye operates the Walt Disney Hometown Museum in Marceline.

Kaye said:

> When children come to Marceline, we'll say, "How old are you?" and they'll say, "Oh, I'm nearly five."
>
> We'll say, "That's the exact age Walt Disney was when he came here." Suddenly it's like an epiphany. They think, "Goodness, he was a farm boy?" Yes. "He did chores?" Yes. And look what happened. Look what he aspired to become. So anything is possible. In Marceline, you truly do know anything is possible.
>
> The Marceline Project was going to be a general living history farm in Marceline, where it all began for him. He wanted to have a working 1900s farm to show people, to get them involved in it, to learn respect for animals and nature. It would have re-created his childhood with the same technology, animals and other elements.
>
> The land had been purchased. The feasibility studies had been done. The governor of Missouri was going to put a four-lane highway in to Marceline. And then Walt passed. We mourned with the rest of the world.

When Walt died, on his desk of his formal office was his concept sketch for the project. Roy took it out of the office and gave it to Rush. Today, it is displayed on the wall of the Disney Hometown Museum in Marceline.

Dave Smith and the Disney Archives had no idea the drawing even existed until it was put on display. It was just another of the many unbuilt dreams of Walt Disney.

The Burbank Disney MGM Studios (1987)

The Disney-MGM Studios theme park in Florida, which first officially opened its gates for visitors in May 1989, was initially planned as an Entertainment pavilion that was proposed for Epcot's Future World section.

This Epcot addition, which was to have been built between the Land pavilion and the Journey into Imagination pavilion, would have featured an exterior that looked like a giant blue sky that hid the show building. Guests would have entered under a theater marquee and pushed themselves through the turnstiles at an old-fashioned movie theater ticket booth.

Once inside, guests could have chosen between taking a ride through a show titled "Great Movie Moments" (Walt Disney Imagineering's first pass at the attraction that eventually became Disney-MGM's Great Movie Ride) or they could board omnimover vehicles through an interactive display designed by Disney veteran Ward Kimball (working with Imagineer Tim Kirk) which revealed the wacky way a Mickey Mouse cartoon was put together. It was tentatively called Mickey's Studio Tour and later Mickey's Movieland.

It was Disney's then-CEO Michael Eisner who first realized that the history of motion pictures really couldn't be crammed into a single Epcot pavilion. He felt it could serve as the basis of a half-day attraction. A half-day attraction is something like WDW's Typhoon Lagoon Water Park, where guests could spend the morning or afternoon there, and then go off and visit some other section of the resort for the rest of the day.

With Eisner's encouragement, the Imagineers greatly expanded their initial concept for Epcot's "Entertainment" pavilion. Using about the same amount of acreage as Disneyland, as well as the same basic design layout of the Anaheim theme park, Disney-MGM Studios theme park came to life.

However, Eisner had vastly underestimated how popular the concept would be. When the studio theme park opened in the spring of 1989, it was immediately mobbed. That was why WDI went into overdrive to quickly "grow" Disney-MGM out into a full-size Disney theme park experience. Among the projects that got immediately approved during the theme park's frantic first years of operation was the Sunset Boulevard expansion project.

Eisner actually seriously considered building at least three more Disney MGM Studio theme parks. The first one was to have been built right next door to what was Euro Disneyland (now Disneyland Paris). However, when that theme park under-performed after it initially debuted in April 1992, this plan was put on hold for nearly a decade, when it finally opened in a severely truncated form in March 2002.

Eisner also tried to persuade the Oriental Land Company (OLC) to allow the Imagineers to build a Japanese version of Disney-MGM Studio theme park as Tokyo Disneyland's second gate. After more than a year of considering the Imagineers' plans, OLC executives rejected the studio theme park proposal preferring to go with a different concept based on the aborted Long Beach Port Disney/DisneySea project that would have been themed to the ocean and they built Tokyo DisneySea.

Perhaps the most intriguing Disney theme park project that was ever proposed was the Disney MGM Studio Backlot, an ambitious entertainment complex that was to have been built in "...beautiful downtown Burbank" right next door to the Disney lot.

It was to be built years before the one in Florida (that had been officially announced in 1985) opened, but using much of the same things developed for that park. Eisner had determined that a West Coast theme park could serve as a more reliable source of income than the fickle film industry.

How close did this project come to becoming a reality? According to a Disney press release the marketing staff released in 1987:

> The Disney-MGM Studio Backlot has been approved and is destined to become the entertainment marketplace of the 1990s. This new generation Disney attraction will be located in the City of Burbank, home to the Walt Disney Studios, and may run a construction cost of $300 million.

It was to be located on a 40-acre site (approximately one-fourth the size of the Florida Disney-MGM Studios) where the ABC Corporate Headquarters, the Feature Animation building, and a multistory parking structure were eventually built.

Again quoting from that press release, Eisner supposedly said:

> Entertainment will be our magnet. The behind-the-scenes Hollywood themes, street performances, live theater, Disney animation tours and operating radio and TV media centers will create an entertainment attraction and shopping and dining experience unlike anything else in the country.

For its Florida park Disney had reached an agreement with the MGM/UA Entertainment Company for the use of film properties from the Golden Age of Hollywood.

Some of those rights owned by Ted Turner—like for the use of James Bond, *The Wizard of Oz*, and *Gone with the Wind*—would have to be negotiated separately, just as they had in Florida. Preliminary plans for Florida's Disney MGM Studios theme park called for a James Bond stunt show, not an Indiana Jones-themed one, but the fee being asked by MGM was considered much too large.

The Great Movie Ride would have featured more of *The Wizard of Oz*, including a scene of being swept to Oz in a tornado, but, once again, it was felt that MGM was charging too much per minute. Disney also obtained rights to other properties from United Artists and Twentieth-Century Fox.

The press release continued:

> We are already developing ideas for special effects thrill rides utilizing the simulator technology we created for Star Tours at Disneyland and night clubs using our 'ghost' techniques from the Haunted Mansion.

A centerpiece of the Disney MGM Studio Backlot project was to have been pretty much a West Coast clone of the Florida theme park's Great Movie Ride, which Eisner described as being the "quintessential Disney adventure ride, totally based on the magic of Hollywood and the movies."

The key difference between the Florida studio theme park and what the Imagineers were proposing for construction in Burbank was that at least one-third of the development's space was to be devoted to retail space. In addition, there would be less reliance on the film properties that had been acquired for the Florida park.

Unlike Florida, WDI's goal was to create the world's first entertainment marketplace where the shopping and dining opportunities would range from traditional and contemporary to the more exotic with specialty shops and street bazaars, so it would be like a hybrid of Downtown Disney and a theme park. Locals would have been able to get into the main section of the mall area for free but the theme park area would be a gated attraction.

In the press release, Michael Eisner said:

> We will enlarge upon the movie-set themes of our Backlot to provide international shopping, dinning and nightlife like Tokyo's Ginza and Paris' Champs-Elysées. We can expand the themes of "lost cities" of the past, the Wild West, California's Gold Rush Days or Disney Fantasy for retail, restaurant and entertainment experiences.

At a later meeting with the City of Burbank, Eisner declared:

> This project will not be a second Disneyland in Southern California. Instead it will be a new generation of Disney attractions.

He didn't want people to think it was an alternative to going to Disneyland; it was called an Entertainment Center, rather than a theme park, in all official documentation.

Imagineers Joe Rohde and Rick Rothschild were put in charge and would later contribute to the Florida version, as well as Pleasure Island. They proposed that the shopping be on the exterior of the property for easy access while the "crazy stuff" would be the center of the complex.

They divided the crazy stuff into four main areas: The Hyperdrome (thrill rides and technology based experiences for young adults), The World of Disney (studio-based entertainment themed to movie making), Cinefantasy (devoted to science fiction, including a museum), and Burbank Ocean (resembling a seaside amusement park with midway games, bumper cars, etc.)

Basically there was 172,000 square feet of themed retail space; 145,000 square feet of restaurants and bars; 94,000 square feet of nightclubs; plus additional square footage devoted to attractions, multiplex screens, and other entertainment venues.

To explain this chaotic mixture, Imagineering created the following back story for the area: In the 1890s, residents of Burbank discovered gold and others flocked to the area building an Old West town. After the gold tapped out, the locals invested their money in making movies and encouraged production by building a backlot complete with a Parisian lane, Spanish street, a California boardwalk, and more. Encouraged by their success, they also built an early radio and television studio. However, the studio and the back lot went out of business and Disney discovered it and transformed it into an entertainment complex.

In some ways, this was similar to the upcoming back story of Pleasure Island, where existing warehouses were re-imagined as nightclubs and shops.

Rothschild told the press that the complex was "where great movies of the past were filmed. The shops, restaurants, nightclubs, and show buildings reuse some of the back lot areas. That way, we could incorporate the variety of all these different themes."

One of the more intriguing aspects for the project was the Hollywood Fantasy Hotel. The Imagineers envisioned it as being the Disney-MGM Studio Backlot's tallest structure. It was a luxurious hotel that was deliberately themed to be a celebration of Hollywood's Golden Age where the cast members who worked at the resort hotel would have worn costumes that made them look like characters from memorable movies.

The 400 individual rooms and suites at the resort would have been designed to look like replicas of famous movie sets. In fact, each floor would have been themed to a different movie genre: film noir, science-fiction, Westerns, etc.

At the very top of the Hollywood Fantasy Hotel, guests would have found the Celestial Dining Room, an elegant eatery that was to have featured a planetarium ceiling. As guests dined, the heavens would seem to rotate, showing guests how the night sky changes as the Earth goes through the calendar year.

To the southwest of the Disney-MGM Studio Backlot project, the Imagineers envisioned building something truly spectacular and unique. On the topmost floor of a multistory parking structure, WDI wanted to build the "Burbank Ocean," a heavily themed outdoor pool area with a pier and massive shipwrecked restaurant. It would have had water cascading 60 feet down the side of that parking structure screening the property from the freeway.

Other entertainment planned for the Disney-MGM Studio Backlot project included a 10-screen movie theater, an ice and roller skating arena, an audience-participation video theater, as well as several heavily themed nightclubs (The Adventurers Club was first developed for here and then later relocated to Pleasure Island in Florida), and restaurants.

Guests were also supposed to be able to tour Disney's historic old animation buildings to see where classic animated films were made and see animators at work. However, a closer examination of the proposed plans shows that a new animation building was to be built for this purpose with animators relocated from their original building. There was to be an archival Disney museum and also soundstages where guests could see current television shows and films being shot.

In addition to all this, all of the scenic areas that the Imagineers were to have created for nightclubs, restaurants, shops, etc. were in theory to have doubled as possible movie sets. It would have been a working Hollywood back lot. The idea being that guests might actually get to see a movie being filmed or their favorite Disney TV show being shot live on location.

The press release closes out by saying:

> All in all the Disney-MGM Studio Backlot will be more than just Lights! Camera! Action!...and Shopping too!

The Disney-MGM Studio Backlot really does have one of the more bizarre back stories ever associated with an aborted Disney project. Universal Studios' intentions were well-known in the outdoor amusement industry that it planned to expand its highly popular Hollywood theme park for an East Coast audience. They had even hired some former Disney Imagineers, like Gary Goddard and Bob Gurr, to help with the designing to create a more tourist-oriented experience.

Universal Studios executives were extremely angry at Eisner at the time when they were ready to firm up an official announcement of the Orlando park. Reportedly, Disney's CEO had "borrowed" many of the ideas for Disney MGM's shows and attractions from a Universal Studios Florida pitch that Eisner had supposedly seen while he was still head of Paramount Studios.

Supposedly, it was one of the reasons the Disney park had a tram tour like the famous one at Universal in Hollywood, as well as stunt and effects shows like Universal as well.

MCA President Sidney Sheinberg would later say about the similarities:

> There was a horrible sense of personal and corporate betrayal. Do you really want a little mouse to become one large, ravenous rat?

Eisner's announcement of a movie themed park in Burbank was meant to discourage Universal from building in Florida and it did end up delaying Universal making a final commitment even though it had already spent nearly forty million dollars. He announced that he wanted to bring the studio backlot theme park idea to Burbank, roughly five miles away from Universal Studios Hollywood, as basically a retaliation for Universal coming to Orlando.

"They invaded our turf, and we're not going to take that without a fight" he said. Eisner supposedly offered to cancel the Burbank plan if Universal didn't come to Florida. Universal firmly refused and when they publicized the offer, both Eisner and Jeffrey Katzenberg vehemently denied it.

As he got involved, Eisner became more and more excited about the idea of the park and thought that similar concepts (but without the "real" studio elements) could be used in Chicago, Philadelphia, and San Antonio.

Universal declared war on the Burbank project. They filed two lawsuits in L.A. Superior Court to stop Disney. Universal even paid for the printing of some anti-Disney-MGM brochures which were then distributed to more than 43,000 people who lived around Walt Disney Studios, talking up how this ambitious project would cause traffic tie-ups, increase tax rates, and more.

Officially the different pamphlets were from the "Friends of Burbank," but were eventually revealed to be from Universal.

While that campaign was annoying, Eisner eventually decided to pull the plug on the project in April 1988, because Disney's accountants told him that the Walt Disney Company would never get a big enough return on its investment.

Costs for the development of the area nearly doubled soaring to more than $600 million and possibly more. Not enough guests to accommodate that expenditure could access the limited area.

In addition, some retailers balked at Disney terms and being part of the project, and even MGM stated that Disney had only licensed the right to use its name for the Florida park and sued to stop them from using the MGM intellectual property in Burbank.

Disney had tried to bully Burbank into selling them the additional land worth $20 per square foot for only fifty-seven cents per square foot, buying the parcel of land worth $35 million (some estimated it as high as $50 million) for only one million dollars total and an option to buy another ten acres at the same price. Disney also wanted Burbank to build a parking structure to hold 3,500 cars that Disney would then rent from the city.

"They promised us the world and then they pulled the rug," said the disappointed mayor of Burbank. The city solicited offers from other developers, including one for a marine park with a massive aquarium. Eventually a simple mall with stores and a movie theater were built.

Disney-MGM Studios in Florida opened in 1989 and Universal Studios Florida opened in 1990.

In 1993, Universal opened CityWalk, a dining, shopping and retail complex that was built right outside of the entrance to Universal Studios Hollywood. While not as elaborate as what Disney had proposed, the complex made a ton of money for Universal and still does today.

Imagineers even took some of the ideas proposed for the Burbank theme park and utilized them in the first version of Disney's California Adventure, including Paradise Pier and its Ferris wheel.

By the way, when the Jaws attraction opened at Universal Studios Florida, there was a boat that had been attacked by the infamous shark. Nearby floating in the water was a set of Mickey Mouse ears with the name "Mike" on them.

Disneylandia (1951)

In the many histories of early Disneyland, some of the books reference Walt Disney's early plans for a little Mickey Mouse Park that would have occupied a mere sixteen acres across the street from the Disney Studio in Burbank.

Sometimes, there may also be a brief mention of Disneylandia, Walt's concept of a series of small dioramas that would travel from town to town via train cars. Interestingly, both projects were being worked on separately at the same time.

Walt's fascination with Disneylandia began with his own love of miniatures that captured his imagination completely in his spare time.

By 1947, Walt was actively collecting miniatures for his own personal collection and even building some examples himself.

In a letter to a friend in 1951, Walt wrote:

> My hobby is a life saver. When I work with these small objects, I become so absorbed that the cares of the studio fade away...at least for a time.

When Walt's collection was inventoried in the mid-1960s, the listing was more than a thousand separate items. Many of them are showcased at the Walt Disney Family Museum in San Francisco today.

However, just collecting these tiny treasures was not enough for Walt. He wanted to create an entire tiny world. It wasn't to be static display to be admired and studied. Walt wanted it to spring to life with movement, sound and light and engage an audience.

In the early 1950s, he asked animator Ken Anderson to draw twenty-four scenes of life in an old Western town in the style of Norman Rockwell's paintings with the same wink of gentle humor that Rockwell did so well.

As Anderson recalled:

> He told me to make drawings that are like Norman Rockwell. "Make them big but make them with a sense of humor. People should chuckle when they see them.
>
> "I'm tired of having everybody else around here doing the drawing and the painting. I'm going to do something creative myself. I'm going to put you on my personal payroll, and I want you to draw twenty-four scenes of life in an old Western town.

"Then I'll carve the figures and make the scenes in miniature. When we get enough of them made, we'll send them out as a traveling exhibit. We'll get an office here at the studio and you and I will be the only ones who'll have keys."

Anderson was given a room on the third floor of the Animation building at the Disney Studio and was paid not by the Studio, but out of Walt's own pocket.

Anderson said:

"I'm going to take you off payroll, I am going to pay you out of my own pocket." He paid me for about a year and then I was put back on the studio payroll. In the beginning, three weeks went by and he had forgotten to pay me. I didn't know what I was going to do. Then he realized he hadn't paid me and he paid me more than I could ever save in my life.

Walt and Ken would sometimes go to downtown Los Angeles searching for materials. Sometimes Walt would disappear for a day or two and then return to Ken's room with, as Ken remembered, "a whole sack full" of various items for this Lilliputian version of his memories of life at the turn-of-the century in Marceline, Missouri and Kansas City, Missouri.

Walt immediately put advertisements in newspapers and hobby magazines seeking vintage miniatures of all kinds for his tableaus. Fearing prices would soar if people heard the Disney name, Walt asked his two secretaries at the time, Kathryn Gordon and Dolores Voght, to use their names in the advertisements rather than announcing that Disney was looking for these items.

Several newspapers and hobby magazines carried the ad:

WANTED: Anything in miniatures to a scale of 1 ½" to the foot or under. Up to and including early 1900s. Give full description and price. Private collector. K. Gordon [and her address].

Walt was constantly having miniatures sent to him on approval then returning them for shoddy craftsmanship or lack of detail. By the time, he had finished work on the first diorama for Disneylandia, Walt had spent more than $24,000 out of his own pocket on miniatures for all the proposed scenes.

Anderson was busy drawing sketches, including a blacksmith reading a newspaper, a minister in a pulpit, a group of gossiping women on a street corner, the interior of a general store and many more vignettes of turn-of-the-century life.

Walt spent countless hours in the red barn in his backyard at home carefully constructing the first of his tiny tableaus. His long, slender fingers, that had served him well as an artist, easily facilitated working with such small objects.

The first scene, titled "Granny Kincaid's Cabin" was based on a set from his live-action feature, *So Dear to My Heart* (1949). It was not an exact duplicate of the actual film set but evoked the same general feeling and time period.

To build the chimney, Walt picked up pebbles at his vacation home at the Smoke Tree Ranch in Palm Springs. To bend wood into the contour of chairs, he borrowed the pressure cooker from the family kitchen.

Inside the cabin, a hand-braided rag rug warmed a floor of planks, not much larger than matchsticks. A china washbowl and pitcher, guitar with strings thin as cat whiskers and a small family Bible sat on the table.

A tiny flintlock rifle hung on the wall, and a spinning wheel with flax sat in the corner. In the bedroom, beyond the living room, was a feather bed four poster with a crazy quilt. The kitchen was equipped with a wood-burning stove and tiny pots and utensils.

The scene looked as if Granny herself had just stepped briefly outside. Granny would not be seen in the completed version. Viewers would simply hear an approximately two-minute recording of her voice describing the cozy scene, for Walt had recorded a narration by actress Beulah Bondi, the famous character actress who played the part of Granny in *So Dear to My Heart*.

Granny Kincaid's Cabin scene was roughly eight feet long, and included rugs, plank floor, stone fireplace, lace curtains, dishes and even an outhouse with a potty.

Imagineer Wathel Rogers said (although the figure of Granny was never constructed):

> The interior of Granny's cabin was completely dressed up with miniatures. Walt made the rocking chairs and the rest himself. He then said, "Let's make up a cross section. Let's have Grandmother rocking, Bible in hand, with a diorama behind her depicting the outdoors. Granny would say, 'Oh hello there, I'm just reading my Bible.' She'd chat for a while, then return to her reading."

In January 1951, Walt contacted a specialist in display cases about an appropriate way of showcasing these scenes. He wrote to the expert that "it always takes a lot of time to work the bugs out of mechanical contraptions and this one must be absolutely right before I can go ahead with the others" but he expected to have a "pretty good show worked up by next Christmas".

In March 1951, Walt asked Harry Tytle, who was sometimes considered "Walt's right hand man" when it came to certain projects and later became a live action film producer, to handle the logistics of the Disneylandia touring show.

According to Tytle's diary for March first:

> Walt called me today and asked how I would like to handle the project [of sending a miniature collection on tour] and when I showed enthusiasm for it, it was indicated it was mine. However, at the time we do not know how it will be set up.
>
> He strongly suggested that, where possible, we give the project a break in costs [this means, accounting-wise, we were to jockey the costs]. We talked of the various talent within the studio that could be used, and how the project would go on tour. Packing boxes, etc. will have to be made; dresses, clothing, etc.

At one point, it was considered calling the show "Walt Disney's America" but the term Disneylandia seems to have been the official title. Walt described it as a series of "visual juke boxes with the record playing mechanism being replaced by a miniature stage setting."

His original idea was to have the exhibit tour the country in railroad cars where schoolchildren would go and visit and place a quarter in a coin box to activate the scene's lighting and sound. At one point, Walt talked about an electric eye triggering the action.

"When I went back on the Studio payroll to work on some animated feature, Walt hired to take my place a guy named Harper Goff and some others," Anderson recalled.

As Harper Goff described it:

> Walt envisioned a big long train which would go all over America. In each city, people would come and go through the railroad cars. They would start at the back of the train, and all the cars would have these little animated things that you could watch.
>
> This is what caused Walt to choose the size he did for the displays. He said he didn't want to build specially wide cars and he wanted to make sure he had an aisle [in each railroad car] with enough room. ... This idea called for a 21-car train on a siding with public access.

Why a traveling show? As Goff told an interviewer:

> [Walt] didn't want poor people to have to come clear across the country and stay in a hotel. He wanted to go to the people. He wanted to have something here [in Burbank] permanently, but he also wanted to put a show on the road. Some of the Burbank City Council sneered at us. They didn't want to bring a carnival to Burbank. They didn't want the kind of people that followed carnivals.

Imagineer Roger Broggie stated

> We started to build what was to be an exhibit of Americana in the same scale [as the caboose for Walt's miniature Carolwood Pacific

backyard railroad] 1-1/2-inches to the foot, or 1/8th the full size. That means the figures would be nine inches tall.

In a letter to his younger sister, Ruth, on December 4, 1952, Walt wrote:

> ...my newest project. Hoping it will become a reality, but at this point it's very much in the thinking and planning stage. ... I've been collecting all sorts of miniature pieces for the past three or four years, with this project in mind. It's been a wonderful hobby for me and I find it is something very relaxing to turn to when studio problems become too hectic.

A challenge facing the project was that the railroads didn't have extra space for this special excursion train, but offered to put in a "Disney spur line" for a rental of $13,000 a month, according to Imagineer Harper Goff.

Walt was taken aback and expected that cities would have been so excited to have the Disney exhibit that they would help cover all or most of this additional cost. It became apparent very quickly that was not going to be the situation.

Another challenge was that moving the train from city to city would be difficult because there were times when it couldn't take a direct route. As Goff described it, "In order to get to Denver, for instance, the train would first have to go to Cheyenne, Wyoming. Then it would have to turn around [on a different railroad, the Colorado and Southern] and go back south to Denver. And they might not have the tracks to accommodate his train all the time."

Walt and Goff visited some railroad cars from the Southern Pacific that were sitting on a siding in a freight yard.

Goff said:

> Walt decided it looked kind of pinched. Just not a very good place for the public.

Walt also debated the safety of having children come to freight yards and explored the possibilities of presenting the show in department stores in the various cities after the dioramas had been transported there by train.

Goff continued:

> As word got out about Walt's plans, prices began to shoot up. Everybody Walt was contacting seemed to think they could make a lot of money off of Disney and his project.
>
> Walt bought three old Pullman cars, just to kind of fool around with. Then, suddenly, when he wanted to get some more, the price had gone up substantially.

Before proceeding any further, Walt wanted to see if the public might be interested in Disneylandia at all.

Granny's Cabin was exhibited at the "Festival of California Living" at the Pan Pacific Auditorium in Los Angeles from Nov. 28 to Dec. 7, 1952. A press release announced that it represented "the beginning of Walt's new miniature Americana exhibit, entitled Disneylandia."

The *Los Angeles Times* from December 1952 reported:

> [It is]an 8-foot long replica of a Midwest pioneer farm home, hand-icrafted (sic) by Disney in every minute detail of structure and the furniture supplemented by objects from historical collections.

It was recessed into a wall at eye level and surrounded by an elaborate frame so it was as if gazing into a painting that came to life. Numerous publicity photos were taken of Walt showing it to actresses Kathryn Beaumont and Beulah Bondi with each of them holding and admiring one of the miniature set pieces.

Walt explained in a 1953 interview:

> This little cabin is part of a project I am working on, and it was exhibited as a test to obtain the public's reaction to my plans for a complete village.

Goff's job was to watch the public's reaction to the scene each day:

> People would watch and watch. They wouldn't go away. They saw the whole show and they stayed for the next one. So the show had to be stopped for 25 minutes to clear out the audience. Walt knew it was a success.

The February 1953 issue of *Popular Science* ran photos of Granny's Cabin under the headline: "Walt Disney Builds Half-Pint History." The accompanying story stated:

> Its purpose is to entertain people of all ages and also to teach them by means of tiny but exact models how life in the United States developed to its present level.

Walt had collected "miniature copies of antique furnishings from all over the country and built others in his studio workshops."

The positive reaction was a huge encouragement to Walt who had already begun work on two other tableaus: a frontier music hall stage and a barbershop quartet.

However, these new dioramas had become more mechanically elaborate than the simple Granny's Cabin, so Walt called in more technicians and artists to help make them a reality. Imagineers Roger Broggie and Wathel Rogers worked on a turn-of-the-century dancer for the stage.

While Walt was not as directly involved in the physical creation of the next two scenes, he would visit the work area constantly and lose track of time so that his secretary would call down to inform them that Walt was already an hour late for his afternoon appointments.

In February 1951, while live-action reference filming was being done for the animated feature *Peter Pan,* Walt used part of the soundstage to set up a massive grid and raised platform stage where he directed actor Buddy Ebsen in a dance routine. Ebsen was at the studio doing some live-action reference work as a dancing pirate for the animated feature.

Margaret Kerry who was performing live-action reference for the character of Tinker Bell at the time remembers being embarrassed when she was introduced to Ebsen because she was wearing her bathing suit that was her costume.

Kerry said:

> It was not pleasant, walking around the soundstage in my bathing suit all day. You never knew who might drop by the set. One day, actor Buddy Ebsen came by the soundstage.
>
> Not very far away, they had a huge grid, made out of wood. There was a lot of activity surrounding it. He was working on it, and there were all these people around it, talking about it and Mr. Disney would come. I assumed that it was for registration, for live people and then how they were going to register to get their animated characters the right size and so on.

Ebsen, like Ray Bolger, was known as an "eccentric dancer" meaning that he did out of the ordinary dancing, including rubbery movements with his legs. Attired with a vaudevillian bowtie, straw hat and colorful suit, Ebsen went through a series of entertaining impromptu tap dances.

He was filmed in 35 millimeter, so that the individual frames could be studied and duplicated using the grid in the background for a small sculpted 9-inch-tall replica wearing the same outfit through a system of cams and cables.

This frontier music hall stage scene included this 1/8th scale, three-dimensional, tap-dancing vaudevillian, and was called "Project Little Man."

This study proved frustrating because Ebsen never repeated his steps the same way and, working at a smaller size, it was even more frustrating having to recreate something as simple as the pants flopping down correctly when a lifted leg returned to the floor.

Ebsen said:

> [Walt] took me to a room [at the studio] where there were seven little guys with aprons and thick glasses working on a contrivance that pulled wires and a little mechanical man that moved his arms, legs, head and mouth.

Sculpted by Charles Cristadoro and connected to a series of cams and gears like a music box, the little figure did indeed move and is considered the beginning of Audio-Animatronics.

Walt was disappointed with the lack of range of expressions on the carved face of the character and explored using plastics instead to make it seem more realistic but was never truly satisfied. Broggie told Walt that in order to accomplish what Walt wanted, the figure needed to be much larger to accommodate all the necessary interior equipment.

Roger Broggie said:

> We built the figure 9-inches tall. We put springs up through the feet of this figure and operated these cables and that made the figure dance. It was very cumbersome. The cam had to have a three-foot diameter for a two minute show, and the controls that went up and down it had to be patterned around that perimeter. And we had to synchronize the sound with the cam.

In June 1951, Walt and his team of designers and technicians began work on a third miniature display—a traditional barbershop quartet crooning the song *Sweet Adeline*. (Goff remembers the song being *Down By The Old Mill Stream* while Imagineer David Mumford claims it was *Oh, Evelyn*. Perhaps all three songs were recorded.)

The singing was to last a minute and a half. The scene would include a barber, customer in a chair, and two patrons waiting by the chair.

One version had one of the waiting customers in a bathtub, much like the Cousin Orville character in the Carousel of Progress attraction. Again, live actors were filmed for reference against the same grid and raised platform used for Ebsen.

Goff said:

> I designed a little barbershop where you could look out the window and look across the street and see things going on. You saw it from the inside. Then we had a newspaper office where they were printing a paper, and you looked out and saw the barbershop across the street.

While Ken Anderson did a sketch for the scene, Goff was brought in to make additional sketches.

He continued:

> I made a little model of the scene. It wasn't a careful model but it was sized right. Their mouths didn't move in that first model I made. My wife Flossie made the clothes out of a very fine silk. I applied a varnish to the moving areas so the material wouldn't wear out too quickly. What I did was the setting...what the barber shop would look like, so you could visualize it. Walt then took it and had other people work on it.

Broggie said:

> When I was asked what it would cost to operate if we had about a dozen of these little sets. ... I said "you'll never pay the

maintenance costs, because everything is so small." And on that basis, the whole project was killed. We got as far as building the guy in the chair and the barber behind him...then the whole job was stopped!

Walt had finally become convinced that only a limited audience would be able to view these tableaus and they would be unable to generate the necessary income to pay for their continued maintenance and operation.

As Broggie recalled, Walt said, "We're going to do this thing for real!"

Both Granny's Cabin and Project Little Man dioramas are currently on display in the Walt Disney Presents attraction at Disney's Hollywood Studios in Orlando, Florida.

Mineral King (1965)

Walt Disney said in 1965:

> When I first saw Mineral King five years ago, I thought it was one of the most beautiful spots I had ever seen and we want to keep it that way.

Harrison "Buzz" Price stated:

> Like everyone who had worked on this stunning project, we believed that Mineral King would have been the greatest winter resort in the world bar none.

How did Walt Disney who produced movies and animation ever get interested in building a unique ski resort?

In 1931, his doctor recommended that Walt take up some type of exercise to help relieve the stress he was experiencing at work. He tried several sports including golf, horseback riding, swimming, boxing, wrestling, badminton and more.

In a January 1935 edition of the *Los Angeles Herald Examiner* newspaper, it stated that Walt and his wife were vacationing at the Ahwahnee Lodge in Yosemite National Park:

> Movie producer Walt Disney and his wife found the winter sports in Yosemite decidely to their liking. It was the Disney family's first experience with winter sports and they were learning to figure skate before they left Yosemite Valley.

It was here that Walt first learned to ski through lessons with Austrain skiing champion Hannes Schroll at Badger Pass where Schroll was head of the Yosemite Ski School. The two hit it off and became good friends.

In 1938, Schroll and his business partners purchased land with the intention of building a ski resort in the east Sierras, near Donner's Summit and the small town of Truckee. The land encompassed an area around two mountains—Hemlock Peak and Mount Lincoln.

Schroll wired Walt in June 1938 to invest money but Walt was unfortunately out of town when the cable arrived and Schroll had to find others to advance the needed funds to buy the land

One year later when Schroll was seeking additional investments to actually build the resort in the style of the great European resorts, he again approached Walt who in turn wrote Schroll a personal check for

$2,500, and became one of the initial stockholders of the newly chris-tened Sugar Bowl Resort. To honor Walt's support and partnership, Schroll changed the name of Hemlock Peak to Mount Disney.

Among the preeminent enticements that drew skiers to Sugar Bowl in those early years were the chairlift up Mount Disney. The Disney lift was constructed and completed in time for the resorts planned December 15, 1939 opening. It marked the first chairlift to be installed in California.

Designed by Henry Howard, the lift was 3,200 feet long and had a 1,000 foot vertical rise and consisted of 13 steel towers and termi-nals that could be raised as needed to compensate for the snow depth. The cost to riders was twenty-five cents for a ride up or two dollars if you wanted to ski down.

Newspaper reporter Bob Blake spotted Walt at Sugar Bowl on January 7, 1940 and reported that "Walt Disney arrived today without Donald Duck and started skiing immediately."

For many Christmas holidays, Walt and his family visited Sugar Bowl. A 1941 photograph shows Walt, Lillian and their seven year old daughter Diane posing with Schroll. Diane later recalled, "I remember that I very much wanted to learn to ski. The highlight of the trip was when Hannes took me up the chair lift, with my parents, on Mount Disney and skied down with me on his shoulders."

A newspaper account from February of 1941 reported that a direc-tor named Ewing Scott had arrived at Sugar Bowl to begin work on a documentary about the history of skiing that was to be produced by Walt Disney. The film was never produced.

Notable Hollywood personalites like Errol Flynn, Robert Stack, Marilyn Monroe, and Claudette Colbert frequented the resort as did many affluent San Francisco citizens. There were "Snowball Special" trains that ferried Hollywood luminaries up to the remote location.

Walt skied at the resort several times with Schroll and fellow Austrian Bill Klein, who directed the ski school until 1957. According to John Wiley, the resort's first winter sports director, Walt once filled in for a bartender at the lodge's bar.

Wiley recalled:

> There was no television in those days, so he tended bar almost incognito for about two hours.

Walt eventually sponsored such events as the Disney Junior Challenge Trophy and the Sugar Bowl Perpetual Goofy Races for chil-dren. In addition to Mount Disney, there are specific runs named the Disney Nose, the Disney Meadow, the Disney Return and the Donald Duck. A modernized lift replaced the original Disney chairlift and is now called the Disney Express.

The Art of Skiing (1941) was a popular Goofy cartoon in the "How To" series. The opening panoramic view of snow covered mountains eventually focused on a rustic ski lodge with a sign in the lower left identifying it as the Sugar Bowl Lodge. It was clearly the same iconic lodge designed by architect William Wurster.

The animated short is filled with gags of Goofy trying to ski from attempting to put on his pants while his skis are already attached to the difficulty of turning around while wearing skis. Of course, Goofy spends much of the cartoon falling down.

Walt's daughter Diane told me:

> Dad really liked the idea of skiing going all the way back to the 1930s. He never skied well and we have funny home movies of him trying. The artists at the studio used some of that as an inspiration for the Goofy animated short.

The yodeling in the short was provided by Schroll as well as the famous "Goofy Holler" of "Wa-hoo-hooey" that was a variation of a yodel and then was re-used in other Goofy shorts.

Rob Kautz, Sugar Bowl's chief executive, began skiing at Sugar Bowl in the 1970s. He became a ski patrolman before working his way up to the resort's top management spot.

Kautz said:

> One evening, Hannes was telling some of us about that trip down to Burbank in the late 1930s to see if Walt Disney wanted to invest in the resort. Disney and Hannes got to chatting about Austria and yodeling, which Disney liked. So Hannes yodeled for him. Disney was greatly impressed and called in his sound guys to record Hannes. That's what ended up in the Disney cartoons. And Hannes always said, "You know what? I was never paid a dime for that!

On December 19, 1941, a presentation of *The Art of Skiing* was held at the Fairmont Hotel in San Francisco as part of the California Ski Association's first annual Skiers Ball. Walt and Lillian attended the event and introduced the cartoon. One newspaper account described the showing as the film's world premiere, but it had in fact been released to theaters as early as November 12, 1941.

Among his many awards, Walt received the Hans Georg Award posthumously in 1967 for elevating the sport of skiing.

The beautiful Alpine town of Zermatt in southern Switzerland is at the foot of the Matterhorn mountain. It was one of Walt's favorite Europeran destinations. Zermatt is known throughout the world for its skiing that thanks to the high altitutde can even be done throughout the summer.

The entire town is a combustion-engine car-free zone with visitors reaching the destination by a rack assisted railway train from the nearby town. In 1958, the town was the site for the filming of the Disney live action film *Third Man on the Mountain* and Walt was in Zermatt for part of the filming. He and his wife stayed at Zermatterhof, the town's oldest and grandest hotel.

It was this visit that inspired him to build a Matterhorn attraction at Disneyland but also reinforced the idea of the viability of a secluded ski resort for the entire family.

In February 1960, the Winter Olympics were held in Squaw Valley as a result of Alex Cushing who met Wayne Poulsen, the original owner of Squaw Valley at Sugar Bowl 1946. Poulsen invited Cushing to open a ski resort in Squaw Valley with him. Within six years of it being opened, the Winter Olympics came to Squaw Valley.

Organizing Committee President Prentis Hale flew down to the Disney Studio to convince Walt to produce the opening and closing ceremonies as well as the nightly entertainment for the athletes for the Winter Olympics. Walt accepted because he had been thinking about building a ski resort with a different slant and this would give him some hands-on experience and observation that he could transfer to his innovative concept.

At the Olympic Games, Walt met Bavarian ski expert Willy Schaeffler, who was later hired by Walt to help scout a location for the proposed Disney ski resort, and Schaeffler confirmed Walt's choice of Mineral King as the best location.

Harrison Buzz Price and his Economic Research Associates (ERA) that had researched the site for Disneyland was also engaged by Walt and some initial areas investigated included San Gorgonio (near Walt's Smoke Tree Ranch home in Palm Springs), Aspen, Mammoth and finally Mineral King.

Walt came very close to a deal to put his resort at Mammoth Mountain. Negotiations started with Andrew Hurley who owned the resort there and the McCoy family who managed the ski slopes at Mammoth Mountain. However, before the deal was closed, Hurley and the McCoys pulled out at the last minute feeling they were not being treated fairly.

Mineral King was roughly half way between Los Angeles and San Francisco. The high peaks surrounding the valley protected it from the wind and made it exceptionally beautiful and compact.

However, it was surrounded on three sides by the Sequoia National Park created in 1890 under the jurisdiction of the U.S. Department of the Interior but excluded from the National Park because of the belief that mining might return to the area.

Mineral King got its name from the prospectors who mined the terrain for ore deposits starting in 1872. Avalanches and disappointing findings made the area a ghost town roughly a decade later by 1882. However, the area soon became the home to campers, hikers, horseback riders and other visitors, some of whom built summer cabins.

Mineral King which was roughly 15,000 acres had been part of the Sequoia National Forest since 1936 but not part of the Sequoia National Park. Even as early as 1949, the area had been under consideration for recreational development as a possible ski resort.

The United States Forest Service published a prospectus in 1965, inviting bids from private developers for the construction and operation of a ski resort that would also serve as a summer recreation area. The proposal by Disney was chosen from a group of six bidders, and on December 17, 1965, Disney received a three-year permit to conduct surveys and explorations in the valley in connection with its preparation of a complete master plan for the resort.

The Disney proposal envisioned an "American Alpine Wonderland" on the floor of Mineral King Valley: a five-story hotel with 1,030 rooms, a movie theater, general store, pools, ice rinks, tennis courts, and a golf course in addition to a hospital, a gas station, a chapel, conference center, heliport and a power station.

Twenty-two lifts (later scaled back to fourteen) and gondolas would scale the eight glacial cirques above the village, leading to ski runs four miles long with drops of 3,700 feet.

And that was just the tip of the iceberg.

Ten restaurants and cafes would be built (each at different price points for guests) including a 150-seat coffee shop perched atop Eagle's Crest Ridge, 11,090 feet above sea level, called Walt Disney's Sky Crown where there would be entertainment and dancing.

For entertainment at one of the other restaurants, Imagineer Marc Davis designed a show with audio-animatronics bears that eventually became the Country Bear Jamboree attraction at Disneyland.

As Imagineer Wathel Rogers recalled:

> After the Mineral King contract had been signed, Walt had an idea for entertainment after people had been skiing. Walt said, "What we are going to do is have a bear band and have them perform two or three programs of entertainment. We'll say that the bears had come out of the sequoias and we trained them to be entertainers."

The cost for the resort was estimated at thirty-five million dollars and it was expected to attract up to a million visitors just the first year when the previous annual total for the area had been closer to twenty-four thousand people.

Eventually, it was decided that the proposed resort would have two hotels, one deluxe and the other a moderate plus a dormitory for cast members accommodating approximately a total of 7,200 people.

In a brochure about the project, Walt said, "When we go into a new project, we believe in it all the way. That's the way we feel about Mineral King. We have every faith that our plans will provide recreational opportunities for everyone. All of us promise that our effort now and in the future will be dedicated to making Mineral King grow to meet the ever-increasing public need. I guess you might say that it won't ever be finished."

To set the resort apart from other ski areas in California, Walt intended it to be family friendly with activities like ice-skating, tobogganing, sleigh and dogsled rides so that skiing was not necessarirly the primary attraction.

In the summer, there would be activities like exploring caves, horseback riding, tennis, swimming and even entertaining wilderness lectures by Donald Duck. In addition, the resort was to be designed to be at least an overnight visit or longer.

Ladd & Kelsey were selected as architects with Marvin Davis, who provided the intitial layout for both Disneyland and later Walt Disney World, supervising the final overall design.

The designer for the ski facilities was Willie Schaeffler who had worked on the 1960 Squaw Valley Winter Olympics. His proposed lifts would also operate in the summer to take guests to hiking trails, fishing lakes and other activities.

Automobile access like at Zermatt would be limited. Guests would park in an eight to ten story underground garage with room for 3,600 automobiles. Generally, guests would get to the resort by small Cog train. Guests would pay to use the train and at one point, it was even discussed to build a monorail.

However, an all season twenty-five mile highway wide enough to handle a lot of traffic was also discussed. A section of that road would have gone through Sequoia National Park, as would have a proposed high-voltage power line needed to provide electricity for the resort.

Walt, who had always been a staunt conservationist and been recognized for his efforts by the American Forestry Association, the National Wildlife Federation and other similar organizations, wanted to keep the natural beauty of the area intact with as little intrusive infrastructure as possible.

Before Mineral King, Walt Disney Productions had garnered 37 awards for its work with nature conservation, and the Sierra Club had made Walt Disney an honorary life member in 1955.

The spring 1966 issue of *Disney News,* stated:

The area's natural character will be preserved by camouflaging ski lifts, situating the village so that it will not be seen from the valley entrance, and putting service areas in a 60,000 square foot underground facility beneath the village.

A press conference was held at Mineral King on September 19, 1966 to announce the plans for the resort. In attendance was California Governor Edmund G. Brown who strongly supported the project and said that state funding of a year round accessible roadway was in the works. Walt was in attendance but appeared pale and often out of breath. Two months later, he would pass away.

The final Disney plan, approved by the Forest Service in January 1969 (and supported by Governor Ronald Reagan, a long- time friend of Walt Disney), outlined a complex of hotels, restaurants, swimming pools, parking lots, and other structures designed to accommodate 14,000 visitors daily.

Reagan said:

> I want to stress as strongly as possible that I am firmly in support of the development of Mineral King as a recreation area. Southern California urgently needs additional year-round mountain recreation areas.
>
> Development of Mineral King will help serve that need.

The complex was to be constructed on 80 acres of the valley floor under a thirty year use permit from the Forest Service. Other facilities to be constructed including ski lifts, ski trails, a cog-assisted railway, and utility installations like water storage tanks and a sewage treatment facility were under a revocable special-use permit.

Disney anticipated opening the resort around 1972. Later when the legal wrangling started, Disney adjusted the estimate to 1976.

In June 1969, the Sierra Club filed a Federal suit in the Northern District of California court to attempt to stop the project fearing that Disney would negatively impact the environment and that such a new expanded roadway through a National Park was illegal to build and not in keeping with the National Park policies.

In an April 1972, four-to-three decision, the U.S. Supreme Court rejected the suit on the grounds that the Sierra Club had not established that it was suffering direct harm as a result of the actions.

In June 1972, the Sierra Club filed an amended suit including the results of several surveys about the environmental impact. The Sierra Club Legal Defense Fund, founded in 1971 to fight the Mineral King resort in court, lives on today as Earthjustice.

Without Walt, public opposition to the development increased and legal battles escalated. Also rising were the costs for the resort itself so Disney kept cutting back to just ten ski lifts and fewer buildings at a total cost of only fifteen million dollars but truthfully, the champion for the resort was Walt himself and without him or Roy around, the rest of the company felt it was not worth pursuing.

Finally, the Mineral King Valley was annexed into Sequoia National Park in November 1978 by an act of Congress and by then, Disney had officially abandoned the project.

For awhile, Disney spent a few years considering reviving the project on private land at Independence Lake, north of Lake Tahoe and created a scale model. Interestingly, the Sierra Club and the Disney organization agreed to cooperate on the environmental study for the project.

According to the *Los Angeles Times* on March 22, 1978:

> Disney project manager Wing Chao accused the state (of California) of trying to sabotage the [Independence Lake] development. Far from expediting its process, state agencies sniped at the development, resulting in delays that cost the company a year of development time, Chao said, and Disney could tolerate it no further.

That ski resort project was also abandoned.

PART TWO

The Lands That Never Were

Before Disneyland, there were amusement venues that had the word "land" in their title including Wonderland, Funland, Joyland, Dreamland, and Marineland. The word was used to suggest visiting an exotic foreign land or some imaginary location like the Land of Oz.

Even the earliest world's fairs, amusement parks and carnivals were often divided into separate defined sections that were sometimes referred to as "lands" to help visitors decide what to see and where to go.

However, it was Disneyland that established the concept of a venue with self-contained, immersive "lands."

The term "land" became so popular that it was often used for nearby retail venues surrounding Disneyland.

Melodyland Theater was a popular theatrical venue across the street from Disneyland before it became the Melodyland Church in 1969. The Vacationland Recreational Vehicle Park was part of the Disneyland Hotel. Burger Land was on Harbor Boulevard as was the Fox Cinemaland movie theater and the Statueland store that sold concrete statuary and fountains. Wonderland Liquor Store was on Katella Avenue.

When Disneyland opened, there were five lands: Main Street USA, Adventureland, Frontierland, Fantasyland and Tomorrowland. The first real new land to be added to the park was New Orleans Square in 1966 followed by Bear Country in 1972. Today, with the opening of Star Wars: Galaxy's Edge, Disneyland has nine lands.

Over the decades other new lands like Discovery Bay in 1979 capturing the spirit of Jules Verne were planned for the limited acreage of Disneyland and other Disney theme parks have lands like Liberty Square at Magic Kingdom and Toy Story Land at Hollywood Studios.

Usually the word "land" now defines an area that has attractions, shops, food, and beverage locations related to the general theme. Disney has always looked to expansion with new lands to handle all the people.

Ironically, the opening of a new land can result in even more guests wanting to visit causing even more congestion as seen by the opening at Disney's Animal Kingdom's Pandora—The World of Avatar in 2017.

The Beastly Kingdom (1998)

At Animal Kingdom dedication in April 1998, Michael Eisner, then-CEO of the Walt Disney Company, read the plaque:

> I think it explains the park the way Walt would have said it, short and concise: "Welcome to a kingdom of animals…real, ancient and imagined: a kingdom ruled by lions, dinosaurs and dragons; a kingdom of balance, harmony and survival; a kingdom we enter to share in the wonder, gaze at the beauty, thrill at the drama, and learn."

At the earliest planning sessions for the park in 1990, there was to be a section devoted to "myth and fantasy" and the animals associated with that theme. The section devoted to imaginary creatures was called Beastly Kingdom.

In Beastly Kingdom, guests would have crossed over a bridge to get to a land where they could take a leisurely boat ride through strange but beautiful scenery featuring imaginary creatures and then strap themselves into a ride that would have them flying and encountering a dragon-like creature.

Today, the same area meant for that land has become the home of Pandora—The World of Avatar. In Pandora, guests cross a bridge to get to a land where they can enjoy a leisurely boat ride through strange but beautiful scenery featuring imaginary creatures or they can strap themselves into a ride where they will fly through the air with a banshee, something that looks like a flying dragon.

In April 1998, at a cast member presentation I attended, Joe Rohde, executive designer and vice president, Creative, for Walt Disney Imagineering talked to the opening team of Animal Kingdom to give them some insight into the history and development of the park:

"The narrative of the park has always been about our love for animals real, imaginary and extinct," said Rohde. "Paleontology is the love of extinct animals. It's an unrequited love. They are dead. They are never coming back.

> We started by designing the fantasy part of the park first. We're Imagineers. We're Disney. We all know griffins, dragons and unicorns and that stuff. We were buying time. We had $250,000 to spend to get going on this project. You can imagine how long $250,000 would last at Disney—about enough to have breakfast on.

While we we're doing that it gave us time to start traveling around the country visiting zoos and begin to make some connections so we could figure out what the zoo conservation part of this whole thing is because it was something we hadn't done before so working on the Beastly Kingdom part first gave us some freedom to do that type of exploration.

For the Beastly Kingdom, you would cross over a bridge into an area divided into Nice, Beautiful and Dangerous. Nice would have had all the pre-adolescent stuff that appealed to kids, like unicorns. Beautiful would have been a little more edgy with minotaurs and things. Dangerous was to take you through the Jabberwock Woods to the dragon.

We went through many different designs and suggestions, but that core foundation pretty much remained the same. The thrill rides would be in the sections designated for dinosaurs and mythical beasts so the real animals would be isolated and not disturbed by them.

The bridge that would have served as the entrance would have been based on the classic Norwegian fairy tale of *Three Billy Goats Gruff*, about three goats trying to cross a bridge guarded by a fearsome troll who lives underneath. At one point, there was a discussion to have three audio-animatronics goats tied up on one side of the bridge and braying to reference the story.

The marketing material stated:

> Beastly Kingdom is the realm of make-believe animals, animals that don't really exist, out of legends, out of fairy tales, out of storybooks. Like our legends and fairy tales about imaginary animals, this land is divided into realms of good and realms of evil.

At one point it was suggested that the land should be called "Beastlie Kingdomme" to give it more of a medieval storybook feeling, but that spelling was quickly abandoned for a variety of reasons, including that it was too closely associated with just European medieval creatures.

In the good realm, there would have been the following attractions:

FANTASIA GARDENS would have been a musical boat ride inspired by the Disney animated feature film *Fantasia* (1940), and similar to Disney family-inclusive theme park rides like "it's a small world."

The boats would have sailed past Mount Olympus, classic Greek architecture like temples as well as floated beneath a brightly colored rainbow archway. Beautiful gardens and fountains decorated the landscape. Mythological creatures like the Pegasus flying horses, fauns and centaurs would have frolicked in the landscape.

According to the Disney press release, the attraction was:

> A gentle musical boat ride through the animals from Disney's animated classic, *Fantasia.* Both the crocodiles and hippos from "Dance of the Hours" and the Pegasus, fauns and centaurs from Beethoven's 'Pastoral Symphony' are found here.

By the way, the *Fantasia* animated segment alluded to in the press release didn't feature crocodiles. It had alligators.

QUEST OF THE UNICORN was to be an interactive walk-through that challenged guests to find and awaken five golden idols (like a golden griffin) scattered through a garden maze in order to find the location of the magical unicorn.

Each idol would provide part of the code necessary for unlocking the far end of the maze where there would be a rare encounter with a beautiful and stately audio-animatronics unicorn in a secluded grotto surrounded by crystal waterfalls and more.

The clues would have been simple enough for children to decipher. Throughout the maze there were additional magical mythological creatures like a griffin.

This good realm would have also included Mother Goose's Cottage that was supposedly a merchandise location.

In the bad realm, there would have been the following attractions:

LOCH NESS TERRACE was a waterfront eatery that would include periodic visits outside in the lake from the legendary sea serpent-like creature known as Nessie.

This was not the silly sea serpent of Disney animated cartoons, but a large, threatening, realistic and monstrous sea creature with several humps that would have frightened sailors. This eatery would have been in a humble hamlet just beyond a forbidding forest and in the shadow of a nearby scorched-stone ruins of a dark castle. There would also have been a Stonehenge-like plaza.

DRAGON'S TOWER was to be the land's looming major icon just like the castles in other Disney theme parks. This thrill ride roller coaster was to be housed in a tall, charred and ruined castle.

The story developed by the Imagineers was that after a fearsome battle that devastated the original inhabitants, the castle had been taken over by a massive dragon as its new home. The jewel-encrusted dragon was very much inspired by the villainous Smaug in Tolkien's *The Hobbit.* Both greedy dragons guarded a vast hoard of untold treasures.

The dragon figure was to be the largest and most sophisticated audio-animatronics creature ever built up to that time. Inhabiting the nearby caves was to be a colony of bats who were also clever thieves.

Hanging overhead as the guests enter this cave-like queue, the bats' whispers would convince the guests to help them in their plans to rob some of the dragon's riches.

Guests would have been strapped into a suspended inverted roller coaster to create the sensation of flying along with the bats on this ill-advised caper in a wild chase through the dark caverns, collapsing ancient castle corridors and even the fabled treasure lair with all its glittering gold. The climax would have been a confrontation with the fiery-breathing dragon, who was not pleased at the attempt to rob him.

The winged dragon would have been the major character icon of the park. DAK's logo even featured front and center the silhouette of a winged dragon marching along with the other animals. McDonald's, a corporate sponsor at the time, released a Happy Meal toy of a purple winged dragon when the park opened. Even a ticket kiosk at the entrance of the park has the head of a dragon.

The Imagineers insisted on keeping those references, as well as a segment of the parking lot designated as "Unicorn", to keep the idea of Beastly Kingdom in the minds of the guests and the Disney executives. A 1998 DAK marketing television advertisement declared "The imagination of Disney gone wild!" and featured a book with a dragon coming to life and breathing fire as part of the promotion of the park.

As work progressed on the park, the cost of caring and maintaining the real animals caused the budget to soar past all expectations. Cuts had to be made in order to finish the park and get it open on time. Nearly 75 acres were eliminated from the Africa section.

It was decided that either DinoLand or Beastly Kingdom could be built, but not both. Since Disney was already investing heavily in its upcoming animated feature *Dinosaur* (2000), Eisner made what he felt was the best decision because a Dinoland could be used to promote the film and would be easier to build.

The budget cuts affected other things as well. One of the sections on the Discovery River Boats was the Dragon Rocks area. As originally planned, as the guests drifted by the area just pass the Oasis bridge, a rocky outcropping seemed to resemble the head of a dragon. Guests would have heard a menacing growl from inside a cave.

Just as the guests moved pass the location, a dragon's head would have lunged out and unleashed a blast of fire seconds after the boat was safely out of range. The dragon would have been a copy of the sleeping dragon designed by Terri Hardin found underneath Le Chateau de la Belle au Bois Dormant at Disneyland Paris.

Basically, it would have been just the front one-third of the dragon placed on a retractable device inside the cave so its head and neck could move in and out of the cave opening.

Melted suits of battered armor and broken swords and lances stuck in the ground would have decorated the landscape suggesting the unfortunate fate of knights who had tried to previously kill the beast.

However, budget cuts resulted in the guests hearing just the growl and then a ball of fire flying out of the cave. After the Discovery River Boats were closed, that effect was turned off although the cave itself could still be seen from the Camp Minnie-Mickey area.

There were other mythological creatures planned for that boat ride. The boat driver would have been worried that the dragon had awoken the Greek sea monster known as the Kraken. The water would begin to bubble and a huge fin would cut through the water as the boat began to rock. Only the driver pulling out a lyre and plucking a tune would put the Kraken back to sleep so it was safe enough to proceed.

Later around the bend, guests would have seen a beautiful white unicorn with a gold horn in a grove of trees, pawing at the ground and nodding its head. The Imagineers were assured that once all the bugs had been worked out in the rest of the new park and it started.generating income that Beastly Kingdom was part of the Phase II expansion and would be built and open by 2003.

To fill the empty space and provide some additional activities for the guests, Eisner, recalling how Mickey's Birthdayland was conceived and built in only ninety days, approved the building of Camp Minnie-Mickey, where guests could meet costumed characters.

In addition, the quickest and least expensive thing to add to a location was entertainment, so two temporary shows that were expected to last a year or two at most, *Festival of the Lion King* and *Pocahontas and her Forest Friends* were installed.

However, after the opening of DAK financial reports indicated that attendance would not grow significantly enough to justify the expense of the Beastly Kingdom's construction despite positive survey reaction from the guests who wanted the area.

The real irony here is that one of the only reasons Animal Kingdom ever got built was that way back in 1993, guests who were surveyed about ideas for a fourth Walt Disney World theme park responded strongly to the idea of being able to see unicorns and dragons.

In 2006, Rohde told cast members:

> Beastly Kingdom is interesting because in a sense you could consider Expedition Everest with the Yeti to be part of the Beastly Kingdom program. Animal Kingdom, as a premise, should be able to sustain more than real biological animals because, when you take the words "Disney" and "Animal" and "Kingdom" and combine them with each other the logic takes you to a place that is *not* just live animals and science and stuff.

We looked at like ten dragon ideas in the process of getting to Expedition Everest. And it's really hard to explain why they take and why they *don't* take. There's a million reasons. I'm sure we will continue to add animals that are part of the imaginary world to Animal Kingdom.

It is the kind of place that should have those kinds of animals. Not just dragons and griffins, but animated animal characters… animals out of fairy tales…other people's imaginary animals… it's not so narrow as like, you know, just dragons and griffins…it's meant to be a broader umbrella than that.

For years, Rohde still kept hope that the area would be built perhaps even as a separate fifth park next to DAK but finally admitted that it would never happen. He now declares that Beastly Kingdom is now more of a "mantra" for what should be included in Disney's Animal Kingdom than a actual physical entity.

Muppet Studios (1991)

It's time to play the music! It's time to light the lights! It's time to tell the story of the Muppet Studios tonight!

In the late 1980s, puppeteer Jim Henson had tired of having so much of his time devoted to business matters. He was in final negotiations with the Walt Disney Company to sell the rights to his famous Muppet characters and become a creative consultant.

Negotiations went reasonably smoothly, although there were still some issues to be resolved. It looked so much like a completed deal that Henson was already at work on a variety of projects for Disney—from a children's live-action television series based on *The Little Mermaid* to theme park attractions featuring the Muppets.

The Disney Imagineers had big plans for a section at the back of the newly opened Disney-MGM Studios for a new "land" to be called Muppet Studios (and at one point, Muppet Movieland). The area would have essentially parodied in classic Muppet style the movie-making traditions celebrated elsewhere in the theme park.

To introduce the public to the idea that the beloved Muppets were going to become part of the Disney universe, *The Muppets at Walt Disney World* was produced as a one hour television special that premiered on NBC on May 6, 1990. Unfortunately, Jim Henson passed away ten days after this episode aired.

The Muppets discovered that Walt Disney World was just on the other side of Kermit's swamp. Naturally, the Muppets decide to explore the vacation destination with all sorts of misadventures including Miss Piggy getting her feet stuck in the cement in front of the Chinese Theater while attempting to make an imprint and at the end of the show all of the Muppets meeting Mickey Mouse in his executive office.

In addition, costumed character versions of Miss Piggy and Kermit riding in a convertible were quickly added to the finale of *Hollywood's Pretty Woman* stage show at the first Theater of the Stars at Disney MGM Studios.

Phase One of the project was to officially open in 1991 with a new 3-D attraction called *Muppet*Vision 3-D*, supported by a parade and some live stage shows like Meet the Muppets (a costumed character show performed in the theater that now houses *The Voyage of *the Little Mermaid* show) and *Muppets on Location: Days of Swine and Roses* (performed outside on a make-shift stage area at the exit of the Muppet*Vision 3-D attraction).

Costumed characters such as Kermit and Miss Piggy would walk around the park, meeting and greeting guests. Signage soon appeared throughout the theme park announcing the new area.

Phase Two would have included an interactive restaurant, The Great Gonzo's Pandemonium Pizza Parlor, and another major attraction, The Great Muppet Movie Ride, among many other delights.

Former Imagineer Mark Eades told me:

> Jim Henson was very involved with the project. He was genuinely interested in doing theme park attractions. His natural curiosity and openness and receptiveness to new ideas made him a perfect fit to work with at Imagineering. He was always a pleasant, fun fellow to be around.
>
> The room always lit up when he was around. It was a two year process from concept to finished production (for Muppet*Vision 3-D). I think Jim liked that it would be something people could see for a long time in an environment like a Disney theme park. I think he also liked doing something new, unique and groundbreaking.

With the unexpected and tragic passing of Henson in May 1990, the contract was still unsigned and challenges arose. As a result, Disney abandoned further development of Muppet Studios. However, one major project was almost complete, and arrangements were made for it to open as planned as a tribute to Jim Henson.

Jim Henson's Muppet*Vision 3-D was one of the very last projects personally supervised by the talented Henson before his untimely death. It was actually finished by his friend, puppeteer Frank Oz, who coordinated a small group of other creative personnel from both Henson and Disney.

Eades continued:

> This popular attraction opened at Disney-MGM Studios in May 1991 after the Henson family were convinced it would be a fitting tribute to Jim. But after they finished their work on it, they told everyone else connected with The Muppets to walk away from Disney. Of course, we also had to get rid of everything else that was Muppets connected like the stage shows and work stopped completely on the Muppet Studios idea.

The first proposal for Muppet*Vision 3-D would have essentially been an introduction to Bean Bunny with all the other better-known Muppets just having cameos. Bean Bunny first appeared in 1986 as the star of the TV special, *The Tale of the Bunny Picnic*.

In 1989, Bean joined the cast of the television series *The Jim Henson Hour*, appearing in both the control room and "televised" portions of the "MuppeTelevision" segments. Henson was later convinced by the Imagineers that the attraction would be more entertaining for guests if it focused on the more familiar characters, but it helps explains why Bean Bunny is still so prominent in the current show.

A merchandise store, Stage One Company Store—designed so its interior looked like a stage set of the lobby of the Happiness Hotel from the movie *The Great Muppet Caper* (1981)—also opened near the exit of the attraction, but all other related projects were cancelled.

In particular, there would have been a restaurant inspired by the famous memorabilia-filled eateries like Planet Hollywood and the Hard Rock Cafe. Called The Great Gonzo's Pizza Pandemonium Parlor, the restaurant would have been operated by Gonzo and Rizzo the Rat. Things would constantly be going horribly (and amusingly) wrong, both offstage and in the dining area itself.

Gonzo and Rizzo would have hired the Swedish Chef to run the kitchen. Guests could watch him making their meals "live" on little overhead television monitors above their tables that would also show clips of the Muppets from their television shows and movies.

Guests would have seen the food fighting back unexpectedly against the Swedish Chef on the monitor as he tried to prepare meals. Armed lobsters would take over the kitchen to prevent being boiled or an animated lump of pizza dough would spring to life and attack the befuddled chef.

Gonzo and Camilla the chicken would get temporarily lost and stuck in the ducts over the guests' tables where the guests could hear their conversation as they frantically tried to find their way out.

The interior walls of the restaurant would have been decorated with Muppet memorabilia (both real and created), just like a famous Hollywood restaurant. The place would also be interactive—at any moment the kitchen doors might explode open in a cloud of chicken feathers and rants from the chef.

Rizzo and his rat friends (with the help of the real serving staff) would deliver meals to the tables on a small model railroad train with flat cars that ran throughout the restaurant.

When the development of Muppet Studios was cancelled, this concept of an Italian restaurant in the heart of Hollywood was transformed into Mama Melrose's Ristorante Italiano.

The Backlot Theater that housed productions like the *Hunchback of Notre Dame: A Musical Adventure* stage show was originally intended as the location for the major attraction at the Muppet Studios, The Great Muppet Movie Ride, announced to open in Spring 1993.

Parodying the Disney-MGM Studios centerpiece attraction at the time, The Great Movie Ride, the ride would have been, as Jim Henson explained it, "a backstage ride explaining how movies were shot... and all the information is wrong."

Guests would have boarded ride vehicles similar to the ones at The Great Movie Ride and would have glided through several movies being made with gag-filled action happening on both sides of the vehicle. Audio-animatronics Muppets would find themselves in classic film scenes.

One scene was a take-off on the popular 1931 black-and-white horror film, *Frankenstein*. In this scene, director Gonzo and inept special-effects technician Fozzie Bear are overseeing a frightened Miss Piggy and Kermit who have stumbled into a mad doctor's lair in the dungeon of an old castle.

The scientist is Dr. Bunsen Honeydew and on his operating table slab is a ten-foot-tall Beaker (with bolts sticking out of his neck), waiting to be brought to life. The set is filled with strange scientific equipment.

Two rats runnng on a hamster wheel would power a generator providing power to the machinery via a cable. Fozzie, holding the two ends of the cable in each hand, would light up each time the machinery sparked.

Fozzie is repeatedly electrocuted accidentally, causing his bow tie to spin, his eyes to light up, and his wiggling ears to emit puffs of smoke.

The next scene would have been a segment from a big screen version of *Pigs in Space,* a popular segment of the Muppet television show. The crew of the interpid U.S.S. Swinetrek (Link Hogthrob, Dr. Julius Strangepork and Miss Piggy) are in the middle of a battle with space "pie-rats" (pirates who are Captain Rizzo the rat and his relatives with peglegs, eyepatches, and laser guns swinging on ropes from a spaceship that looks like a Spanish galleon). Both groups are wildly blasting lasers at each other.

Yet another scene would have parodied *Peter Pan,* with Kermit (as Peter) teaching the Darling children to fly through a cardboard cut-out set of London. The Darling children would have been Janice (the hippie singer with Dr. Teeth & The Electric Mayhem) as Wendy, the ever-proper Scooter as the bespectacled John, and Fozzie Bear as Michael in footie pajamas and holding a teddy bear.

Rat technicians clearly operate the awkward and obvious pulley rigs and ropes to help these performers fly. However, they are having difficulty with the robust Miss Piggy dressed as Tinker Bell, who from the huge holes in some of the scenery has apparently had some mishaps, so the massive Sweetums has been brought in to try to help control her rope.

There would have been a multitude of gags, including the caustic Statler and Waldorf in a studio golf cart appearing by the side of the ride vehicle every now and then to offer their typically sarcastic commentary before disappearing backstage.

The area outside the attraction, including the storefronts, would have been themed to the Muppets. Fire Station No. 1 (the home of the fire truck that appears at the end of Muppet*Vision 3-D) still exists today. At one time, even the actual fire truck from the scene was on display nearby and then later moved to the Studio Backlot Tour.

Philo's Fish Co. next door was originally intended to be Lew Zealand's Boomerang Fish Market. Guests walking along the street would have heard the performer practicing.

In the windows would have been fish packed in blocks of ice that would spin around or offer awful puns like being "hard of herring." All of this was only just the beginning of the fun to be discovered by eager guests at the shops along the street.

One of the few remnants of the Muppet Studios is in the pre-show area of Muppet*Vision 3-D, where crates are clearly addressed to be delivered to the Muppet Studios, not Muppet Labs that has created the 3-D theater and experience.

In 1991, Disneyland president Jack Lindquist had made plans for the Muppets to take over Disneyland and make it into Muppetland because the regular Disney characters would be on a year long vacation since they were exhausted from hosting the previous year 35th Anniversary celebration.

Full page advertisements would have shown Mickey handing over the keys to the park to Kermit. The Disneyland entrance marquee would have been changed to say "Muppetland". The famous flowerbed at the front of the park with Mickey's head in flowers would have been replaced with a Kermit head.

Various Muppet characters would have popped up in cameo appearances in the Disneyland attractions including Miss Piggy as Cleopatra in It's A Small World and Animal in Pirates of the Caribbean partying with the scoundrels and knaves. It was even suggested to paint the Matterhorn green.

Like in Florida, there would have been parades and stage shows. When Henson passed away and there were challenges in contract negotiations, all of these plans were abandoned.

Disney made a licensing agreement with Jim Henson Productions to continue using the Muppet characters for the 3-D attraction which is how it was able to premiere at Disney California Adventure in 2001.

Disney finally acquired the Muppets intellectual property (except for the Sesame Street characters) for seventy-five million dollars on

February 17, 2004. The original contract with Jim Henson was for a hundred and fifty million dollars but the Muppet brand had lost a lot of its sheen after Henson's passing.

Disney formed the Muppets Studio (originally called the Muppets Holding Company) as a wholly owned subsidiary responsible for managing the characters and the franchise. Muppet is now a legal trademark of the Walt Disney Company.

After acquiring the Muppets, one of the earliest plans that never happened was to transform the unpopular dark ride at Disney's California Adventure into Miss Piggy's Superstar Limo.

In this version, guests would board limousine ride vehicles for a trip through a "Muppet-ized" version of Hollywood and arrive at a big premiere of a film starring Miss Piggy. The plan was for the ride system to remain the same as well as the ride vehicles and the track layout but to totally redo the scenes.

WDI pitched that Disneyland's Space Mountain be renovated as the Muppets' Pigs in Space Mountain based on *The Muppet Show* segment. The U.S.S. *Swinetrek* would jut out the side of the cone-shaped mountain as if it had crashed into the iconic structure. Throughout the queue on overhead monitors, guests would have been told that they are about to join Miss Piggy, Captain Link Hogthrob, and Dr. Julius Strangepork on a dangerous space mission.

They have to deliver a pepperoni pizza to the Supreme Galactic Leader in thirty minutes or less, just like the famous motto of Domino's Pizza. If they don't, then not only is the pizza free but the universe faces total annihilation. For cost reasons, most of the Muppet appearances would have been just on the monitors before boarding the attraction, but WDI hoped to be able to get three-dimensional figures of the crew somewhere inside.

Currently, the company has no plans to revive the idea of a Muppet themed land at a Disney theme park.

Today, at Disney's Hollywood Studios there is a Muppet Courtyard with the Muppet*Vision 3-D attraction, the former Pizza Planet quick serve food and beverage location transformed into PizzeRizzo and the Broadway Plumbing bathrooms renamed Gonzo's Royal Flush Executive Used Toilet Showroom (inspired by Gonzo's business from the 2011 movie *The Muppets*).

Roger Rabbit's Hollywood (1990)

As part of the plans for Disney CEO Michael Eisner's announced Disney Decade, one idea that had been discussed for Disneyland was to convert the area behind Main Street U.S.A. into a Hollywood Land with a section featuring some attractions devoted to Roger Rabbit and his cartoon friends who had become hugely popular with the release of the feature film *Who Framed Roger Rabbit* (1988).

In May 1991, Disney officially cancelled the project claiming in a statement to the *Los Angeles Times* that the primary reason was that "proposed construction would come at the same time as development of the proposed WestCot theme park nearby."

These same Roger Rabbit elements that had been developed by the Imagineers were suggested for an expansion at the Disney MGM Studios to be located approximately where Sunset Boulevard is today.

When Disney MGM Studios opened in 1989, it was meant to be a half-day experience but it instantly became so hugely popular that Disney immediately started developing plans for expansion that eventually led to the opening of the Sunset Boulevard in 1994.

Known as Roger Rabbit's Hollywood (and sometimes as Maroon Studios, the fictitious animation studio where Roger works), it would have been an entire street that looked as if it belonged in Toontown with its wacky architecture. Guests would have been able to visit the massive ACME warehouse filled with gags. It was an area that was later incorporated into the exit of the original Studio Backlot Tram Tour.

Later versions of the concept had it confined just to the end of Sunset Boulevard near where the Rock'n'Roller Coaster is today.

An often quoted *New York Times* article from February 18, 1990 stated:

> Disney's movie division is providing inspiration for a new series of back lot 'neighborhoods', rides and restaurants at Disney-MGM Studios in Florida. According to plans for the theme park announced recently, the movie *Who Framed Roger Rabbit* made by a Disney subsidiary, Touchstone Pictures, will be the source for an area called Roger Rabbit's Hollywood to be built in the mid-1990s.
>
> This will be a kind of Toontown, where—as in the movie—only cartoon characters may live.

Visitors will meet the movie's eponymous cartoon hero, ride a Toontown trolley rocked by flight simulators, hop into Benny the cartoon cab, and careen in overaged Baby Herman's baby buggy through a Toontown hospital.

The street would be littered with all sorts of traditional cartoon gag surprises like boxes of TNT, a grand piano dangling precariously over the street, and Roger-shaped holes in the walls.

Red Cars would take guests up and down the street and stopping at the Terminal Bar from the movie where Dolores worked that would serve as the main restaurant for the new area. In addition there were plans for a smaller Toontown Diner which would have been a quick serve location.

The Toontown Trolley attraction would have been a motion control simulator like Star Tours with some differences, including not only a screen in front but on each side. There would be in-cabin effects like Roger shaped dents that would appear when the character crashed into the roof.

Baby Herman's Runaway Baby Buggy would have been a traditional Fantasyland-like dark ride. It would be based on the incidents in the first Roger Rabbit short, *Tummy Trouble* (1989) where Roger and Baby Herman had a series of misadventures in a hospital. Guest would have boarded oversized baby buggy ride vehicles and then careen down stairs, through hospital rooms, around beds and patients and more.

When the attraction was described in the newspapers, some readers angrily complained that there was nothing funny about a hospital and that the Disney Company was being insensitive to both patients (especially scared children) and doctors, especially since the short featured frightening sharp objects and scary mechanical devices.

Benny the Cab was an attraction planned for the area that did get tweaked and built later as Roger Rabbit's Car Toon Spin at Disneyland Park in January 1994. Because Disney and Amblin both co-owned the new characters in the original film and were having a dispute, Benny was transformed into his "twin cousin" Lenny. Imagineers tried to explain the missing Benny by saying that Roger was out driving him at the time so he was unavailable.

Elements of Roger Rabbit's Hollywood as well as ones from Florida's Mickey's Birthdayland/Starland were later developed into Mickey's Toontown at Disneyland.

The Equatorial Africa World Showcase Pavilion (1983)

Imagineer Ken Anderson was the principal designer for the planned Equatorial Africa pavilion that was to be at the World Showcase at Epcot.

Equatorial Africa refers to the group of African countries that lie along the equator. During its development, this pavilion was also referred to as the "African Nations pavilion" and just the "Africa pavilion".

The pavilion was to be located between the China and Germany pavilions roughly in the area where the Outpost (originally called Village Traders in 1993) is today.

When Epcot Center opened, entertainer Danny Kaye hosted a CBS television special on October 23, 1982, celebrating the new park. Standing with author Alex Haley who was the show writer for the pavilion in front of the location where the Africa pavilion was planned, Kaye commented that he was eager to return in a year to tour the impressive pavilion that would then be opened.

A scale model of the pavilion was shown to tantalize viewers. There were signs in the area promising that the "Dark Continent" would be coming soon.

While several other pavilions had been promoted as joining the World Showcase soon, Equatorial Africa was the most developed, as evidenced by the conceptual painting of Epcot Center by artist Clem Hall who featured it in the original World Showcase section.

Anderson was primarily in charge of the development team that also consisted not only of writer Haley but also artist Herb Ryman and cinematographer Jack Couffer.

One of the reasons long time Disney artist Ken Anderson was put in charge of design was because of his inspirational sketchbooks from his time spent in Africa. They feature a great attention to detail to capture the true spirit of the place. These sketchbooks were shared with the appreciative team of designers working on the pavilion.

Ryman specifically asked to be part of the design team and painted a number of inspirational acrylic paintings that still survive today. Ryman also went on an artistic safari to Africa in February 1983, encountering many adventures along the way in his desire to be able to paint the real thing.

He traveled throughout Africa, spending time in such places as Nairobi and Lake Naivasha, Kenya, and East Africa. He befriended Haley and they remained friends up to Ryman's death in 1989.

Ryman, who at one time painted a portrait of Haley, said:

> When my friends who have never met Alex ask me my opinion of him, I can only say, There probably is somewhere in the world another man who is as noble a soul, as genuine and sincere, and as loving and caring for all things, both great and small, as Alex Haley but I haven't met him yet.

> Alex Haley was telling me at lunch, "I'm just a bystander, but it's fantastic to see the way people don't walk when they come in [to Epcot], they don't run, they race to where they want to go. They just race...it's a fantastic thing."

Ken Anderson added:

> He was a remarkable storyteller and when he spoke, he was mesmerizing. His storytelling talents, combined with the artistic talents of the team would have made a potentially powerful showcase for the African continent.

> [They wanted with the pavilion] to explore the exotic continent of Africa using the elements of art and rhythm in an open village atmosphere. Guests would experience the wide variety of African landscapes including indigenous plants from the arid and sandy coastlines to the grassy savannahs to the lush and thickly forested jungles.

The team worked intently for over two years on designing the pavilion. The guest experience was to begin with an imposing and fascinating 60-foot-tall tree house. Imagineer Pat Burke remembered that when he did a model of the tree for the World Showcase as part of the overall model, Imagineer John Hench complained it was too big in scale and needed its own theme park.

It overpowered the other World Showcase pavilions. Some believe that tree helped inspire the centerpiece Tree of Life at Disney's Animal Kingdom Park. Burke did several sizes of the tree to try to bring it into scale.

Set high in the branches of this giant man-made Ficus tree, was a wooden observation platform that surrounded the upper trunk. From the center of this platform, guests could overlook a watering hole at dusk with the slightly darkened lighting adding to the overall illusion.

Jack Couffer, a cinematographer and director who worked on several of the Disney True Life Adventure films of the 1950s and 1960s like *Secrets of Life* (1956), filmed extensive footage in Africa for use in the pavilion, as well as for reference.

Couffer was responsible for many Disney nature-related films including *Nikki, Wild Dog of the North* (1961) and *The Legend of the Boy and the Eagle* (1967). After working at Disney for roughly about a decade on about two dozen films, Couffer went on to other projects including an Oscar nomination for his work on *Jonathan Livingston Seagull* (1973).

The wild animals were presented on film, but the experience was to be more than just visual. It was to be an immersive adventure with heat and wind, scent (using Disney's smellitzer technology) and sound (like running water), so that there was an atmosphere of drama being recreated as animals confronted each other at the watering hole as they came to bathe or drink. The intention was to create the illusion that the guest was actually in Africa and catching a glimpse of the wild animals.

Of course, using real animals in such a confined setting would have been challenging for a number of reasons. So there was a 20-foot tall panoramic screen that would have encircled the area, and the 70mm live action footage of wild animals that Couffer shot would have been rear projected on it.

The screen would be obscured in places by fake trees, rocks, vines and more in the foreground and the fading light of dusk setting would have helped mask the fact that it was movie. More than 100 different animal scents, including lions in heat, had been planned to be sprayed into the air.

Leaving the tree house, guests were faced with massive granite rocks (Kopjes), which served as the framework for an outdoor amphitheater. Kopjes rise up from the sea of grass on the veldt in the Serengeti-like little heads. The rock-enclosed theater was to be a natural setting for live entertainment provided by native African dancers and musicians.

Anderson said:

> These performers would be from many different tribes from all over Africa and would demonstrate the colorful traditions from their specific areas and the action could be viewed from many different perspectives.

Next to the amphitheater would be a huge thatched dome. Inside the structure, guests would enjoy *Heartbeat of Africa,* a show focusing on the rhythms and music of Africa. Anderson kept referring to it as the "Rhythm Show".

Guests would have leaned back on replicas of huge, colorful tribal shields in a darkened room filled with instruments covering the walls and ceiling. There would be a pre-show film about the importance and history of the drum in Africa.

Drums magically played themselves and "with each hypnotic beat, light would emanate from the instrument." Gradually, the rhythms would become more complex and more and more instruments would join in with the elaborate melodies "causing the room to be filled with colors, patterns and music."

It was a jazz concert in a modern African city with laser images coming out of the instruments. The guests would have felt completely surrounded by all this sound and color.

When the guests left the show, they would see across the village center two enormous elephant tusks crossing each other to form an archway high enough and wide enough for guests to walk under into a colorful native shopping area filled with performers: "Native art, such as carvings, masks and jewelry as well as many of the instruments seen in the Rhythm Show would be available for purchase".

In addition, there would be large portrait posters of animals observed in the tree house and that would be heard in the walk-through Sound Safari that was nearby. A small museum area featuring a rotating collection of African art was also proposed for this heritage section.

On the Sound Safari walk-through, guests would have experienced an African adventure through a sense of sound. Walking on a meandering, overgrown footpath over a suspension bridge and through dense jungle thickets, guests would encounter hippos, crocodiles, a herd of elephants, hyenas, wild dogs, lions and exotic birds...but only through a sense of sound.

Infra-red sensors would trigger off the sounds of trumpeting elephants and grunting hippos and other African animals also causing the foliage to move as if these animals were just beyond the sight of the guests.

The realism would be increased by the rustling of the upside-down Baobab trees and other ambient sounds from the jungle that would have meshed with "special effects that infer the presence of animals. The climax would be a trip through a dark, cavernous lion's den during a feeding frenzy over a fresh kill."

The final show at the pavilion was titled *Africa Rediscovered* and was written and hosted by Alex Haley. It was a fifteen minute widescreen film presentation. The pre-show began with a giant relief map of Africa and then a brief film showcased the natural wonders of flora, fauna, and climate.

Anderson said:

> The purpose of the main show was to dispel the myth that Africa had always been a jungle inhabited by wild beasts, savages and Tarzan. The facts show that Africa has had a long and illustrious history. Wealthy empires and enlightened scholarly cities have existed there for many centuries. There have been times in the past when African cultures were more 'civilized' than their European counterparts.

The film began with Haley himself in the Sahara Desert explaining that he would be the guide through the history of Africa. "Africa—the Dark Continent. It's been called that, not because most of the people who live here are black, but because knowledge of it is shadowy," Haley said.

He visited the ruins of Kush, a little known Nubian civilization located a 1,000 miles south of ancient Egypt. He wandered the rubble and the long-deceased civilization is magically restored (thanks to movie magic) to its glory in 750 B.C.E. Haley witnessed some of the great events of this forgotten kingdom.

Next, Haley was high in the Alps. One frightening segment showed an elephant with riders slipping off a crumbling, narrow pathway high in the Alps and plummeting to its doom along with its human riders.

"It was through these snowy passes that Hannibal, the Black ruler of Carthage, trekked with his army and teams of elephants," Haley remarked.

Carthage was a wealthy trading center and one of the greatest cities of ancient time, located on a peninsula in North Africa.

Haley said:

> Carthage controlled an empire, and the Carthaginians were more interested in trade than in conquest. But they used military power when they felt it was necessary, so Hannibal led his army on an unprecedented and audacious trek through these Alps to fight against Rome and protect Carthaginian interests in Sicily.
>
> Hannibal persevered against tragedy and overwhelming odds, and although he lost the final battle at the gates of Rome in 201 B.C.E., he was called the 'Greatest General in History' by Napoleon Bonaparte.

Haley next appeared in modern Timbuktu surrounded by richly clad people with colorful robes and impressive displays of gold earrings and assorted jewelry.

Haley states that in its heyday, Timbuktu was known as "The City of Gold" and, as he said it, the area was restored to its ancient glory when it was the crossroads of the medieval world's gold and salt trade, the center of education and the site of the world's first university while Europe was still mired in the Dark Ages.

However, Haley pointed out that the main source of gold for Asia was Zimbabwe in South Eastern African and he found himself in the ruins of that trading center.

Zimbabwe was the hub of a large confederacy of 400 nations and traded in frankincense, ivory, ebony, and iron, as well as gold. Haley admired some of the finest gold sculptures produced in a city that existed before the birth of Jesus.

The film then transitioned to Haley admiring the magnificent bronze sculptures of Benin, a wealthy trading center of Africa's west coast and the home of bronze art. Haley was escorted through the present day palace of the Oba (or "King"). A young member of the court took Haley through a great collection of bronzes that foretell the disaster that befell Benin's civilization with depictions of European firearms and slavery.

Haley then visited, in quick succession, many other African cultures that evolved before the time of Jesus, including Egypt, Axum, Carthage, Ghana, Mali, Songhai, Kanem, Bornu, Kilway, Lamu, Zanzibar, Engaruka, Bunyoro, Kongo, Asante, and, finally, Abyssinia.

He pointed out the one thing they all have in common with Benin was that their cultures and history were destined for destruction and oblivion by greed and slavery.

Haley then appeared in the slave prison of Goree off the west coast of Senegal. He groped through the musty corridors and peered into the gloomy vacant cells. Slaves seemed to appear once more in manacles and Haley learned how a mercenary system established high prices for slaves.

He discussed how slave hunters, armed with firearms, drove deeply into the country, sacking villages and towns and how greed prevailed and was the underlying motive behind capturing slaves. He mourned that whole civilizations were uprooted and hundreds of thousands of Africans were killed or sold and much of the continent was decimated by the slave trade.

He then told of Ann Zingha, the fighting Queen of Angola, who spent 16 years battling slavery. Unable to get men, she recruited and trained Angolan women to fight with bows, arrows, spears and clubs and successfully held off heavily armed foreign troops for a decade and a half before finally being defeated. With her defeat, the last of the great old civilizations were gone.

When 19th century colonists arrived in Africa, they found civilizations broken and in disarray because of a 100 years of slave wars.

Haley summed up that the myth of a "Darkest Africa—an uncivilized continent peopled by savage tribes" was untrue but the myth still prevails today. He states that the opposite of the myth is what is true, that past African cultures were many and illustrious.

He enthused that Africa, the world's second largest continent, four times the size of the continental United States with 96 percent of the world's diamonds, 65 percent of the world's gold, more uranium than all the rest of the world combined, untold oil reserves and now equipped with modern technology—is prepared to take its rightful place in the family of modern nations.

That was a lot of material to cover in just fifteen minutes.

Why was the pavilion never built?

Companies who operate in the specific countries represented in the World Showcase had to put up the lion's share of the money to finance the construction and maintenance of the pavilion. At the time in the early 1980s, that cost was roughly $30 million.

Supposedly, the only African corporations willing to come up with that kind of money were based in South Africa, where the practice of apartheid was being spotlighted in the world arena.

Disney did not want to be associated with that racist policy. In addition, there was constant political upheaval in Africa with coups and wars changing leaders and policies, as well as the representatives that were negotiating with the Disney Company.

In addition, while EPCOT Center opened strongly, attendance dropped off rapidly and significantly. Disney management had to consider whether money should be invested in what was perceived as another "boring" educational pavilion or in some other more exciting attraction.

Certainly, the concept artwork, scripts, film and more still exist today. Many African artifacts were purchased and some of those ended up at the Adventurers Club at Pleasure Island. Disney Architect Ahmad Jafari worked on both this proposed World Showcase pavilion and Disney's Animal Kingdom Park and some of the designs also re-appeared in Adventureland at Hong Kong Disneyland.

When Animal Kingdom opened in 1998, I talked briefly with Imagineer Joe Rohde and remarked that since Africa was represented in the new theme park, that it meant that the concept for a pavilion representing Africa would never be built at World Showcase.

With more than a hint of surprise, Rohde answered:

> Jim, you don't understand that it is two different stories. The story of DAK is about animals real, imaginary and extinct. The story of World Showcase is about people and their cultures. I would love to see an Africa pavilion at World Showcase.

As others point out, Africa is, in fact, represented at the World Showcase today. When negotiations finally broke down on the pavilion, the King of Morocco, a country on the northwest part of Africa where the city of Casablanca is located, had the nation's government sponsor its own pavilion, and even had artisans go to Florida to help in the design and building of the pavilion. It is the only pavilion at the World Showcase that is sponsored by the government of that country.

World Showcase Pavilions (1983–1988)

The original plans for this shoreline version of World Showcase presented four years before the area opened were significantly different.

Card Walker, president and CEO of Walt Disney Productions, announced October 2, 1978, to delegates of the 26th World Congress of the International Chamber of Commerce meeting at the Contemporary Resort Hotel that the upcoming E.P.C.O.T. Center would consist of two major themed areas: Future World and the World Showcase.

Attending that event were thousands of the world's business elite, along with President Jimmy Carter, former Secretary of State Henry Kissinger, and Florida Governor Reubin Askew.

Walker said:

> The World Showcase will be a community of nations, the only permanent international exposition on the culture, traditions, tourisms and accomplishments of people around the world. A model for true people-to-people exchange, the World Showcase will offer participating nations an opportunity to send their outstanding young adults to operate the attractions, shops, restaurants and exhibits of their pavilions. And these young people who will work, play and learn together for a period of up to one year will help to generate greater international understanding.
>
> We have received letters of intent from business or government interests in ten nations for participation in the first phase of the World Showcase—including United Mexican States, Japan, Federal Republic of Germany, Kingdom of Morocco, Canada, State of Israel, United Kingdom, French Republic, United Arab Emirates and Italian Republic. And in the months to come we anticipate substantial additional support for the planned second phase.

Second phase? Well, the World Showcase was planned to open with ten pavilions as just the first phase of the project, with additional country pavilions to be added within the first five years—including one devoted to Spain and another to Equatorial Africa.

Here are the original official descriptions of the pavilions reflecting that even the pavilions that finally did appear in 1982 underwent significant changes.

UNITED MEXICAN STATES: The Mexico Pavilion is a reflection of the country itself: a country boldly moving into the future without losing touch with its proud heritage. The pavilion's fair weather entrance exposes guests to a modern interpretation of an ancient Indian pyramid against the background of the main show building, which has an enormous mural, covering the entire front of the structure. As guests pass into the pyramid, they find that the polished gold exterior is, in reality, made of mirrored windows that reflect the sun's searching rays. At night, the effect is reversed and the pyramid becomes a shining beacon of light. This is the first of many surprises that await guests in the Mexico pavilion. The highlight of the pavilion is a water excursion with colorful boats themed to the famous Xochimilco Gardens. They convey guests through the history of Mexico.

FEDERAL REPUBLIC OF GERMANY: Guest entering the German pavilion of World Showcase will find themselves in a spacious plaza surrounded by ornately decorated buildings representing traditional as well as contemporary German goods. A glockenspiel with life-sized animated figures adorns the plaza clock tower and a sculptural fountain depicts the well-known story of St. George and the Dragon.

The plaza ramps down to a sunken courtyard where guests can enjoy a snack and a view of the boarding area of the German Rivers ride, a simulated cruise down Germany's most picturesque rivers: the Rhine, the Tauber, the Ruhr and the Isar. Guests will ride past intricately detailed miniatures of famous landmarks including Neuschwanstein Castle, the Garmisch Ski Area, Rothenberg and the Cologne Cathedral.

The miniatures will be scaled so that they will appear to be full sized scenes viewed from a distance. In addition to the miniatures, the ride will feature several life-sized tableaus which will appear as animated visions in the sky. These tableaus depict milestones in German history and culture. The ride debarks at an authentic beer garden where guests can enjoy food, drink and music in the most festive of German settings.

JAPAN: The entrance to the Japan pavilion is marked by a traditional wooden archway, located along the shoreline of the World Showcase lagoon. Guests will walk past a ceremonial temple bell and an ornately decorated pagoda before arriving at the pre-show area for a carousel theater show entitled, *The Winds of Change*. (Later changed to *Meet The World* and sent to Tokyo Disneyland.)

Through the magic of audio-animatronics and film, this four-act show traces the major influences on Japanese culture from the earliest Chinese visitors to the present. The show concludes with a multiple screen film presentation depicting modern Japan's vast manufacturing output and its impact on the rest of the world.

Exiting the carousel theater, guests will be greeted by neon lights and music typical of the Ginza, a recreation of downtown Tokyo's famous nighttime shopping and entertainment district.

FRANCE: Paris is the heart of France, and this city's street life and flavor, which revolve around the River Seine, are captured in the French pavilion. Guests can walk along the waterfront's tree-lined embankment. Above them, the promenade is lined with bookstalls and poster kiosks. This boulevard borders an outdoor cafe where guests dine under brightly colored canopies. The cafe itself is located in the foreground and interior of a handsomely arcaded building modeled after the Rue de Rivoli. Leaving the entrance area, guests walk the street and stairway leading to Montmartre—the artists' quarter of Paris.

UNITED KINGDOM: Green lawns, ornamental gardens, gable roofs, and spires form the setting for romantic expectations. The promenade separates an English pub from the main body of the pavilion. Its shoreline location affords its guests a scenic view over a River Thames and canal setting. Across from the pub, shops and an Albert Memorial style information booth line the main village thoroughfare.

The iron and glass work of St. Pancras or Victoria Station is recalled in the structure of the train shed. Nearby, guests can walk through passenger cars where scenes of the British Isles are re-created through the car's windows. Exiting the train, guests may enter a 200-seat theater for a traveling film presentation on the United Kingdom.

ISRAEL: On the shorelines of the Israel Pavilion, the ruins of an ancient minaret serve as an information center. Olive and cypress trees line the entrance and provide shade for buildings and traveler alike. Beyond the pavilion's entrance, the rising walkways lead travelers to a courtyard setting with shops clustered around the perimeter. The bazaar atmosphere of a marketplace in Israel permeates the interior and exterior of the shops. Tapestries, custom wood and brass items, jewelry, fashion apparel, and quality gifts provide guests with a small piece of Israel to take home.

CANADA: The Canada Pavilion is based on an outdoors theme that re-creates the majesty of the Canadian wilderness: roughly cut log dwellings, river gorges, steep mountainsides. All roads converge on Salmon Island where the rugged natural beauty of the Canadian outdoors stands alone. Waterfall, all pine trees and an abandoned mine tunnel seem to mark a dead-end until a waterfall magically parts and a drawbridge extends out, beckoning guests into the Canadian Circle Vision Theater. Here guests will be surrounded by nine screens for the spectacular film *Canada the Beautiful* in Circle Vision 360.

ITALY: The classic grace of Italy's art and architecture form the backdrop for the World Showcase's Italian Republic Pavilion. Colonnades, gardens and shops are overlooked by a restaurant featuring cuisine in the grand Italian tradition. The guest enters from a stone footbridge modeled after Venice's pedestrian bridges.

Gondolas are docked nearby, an obelisk rises from the center of the courtyard, and from here guests can see recreations of some of Italy's greatest Renaissance buildings. Shops feature examples of time-honored Italian workmanship. One area of the pavilion will be set aside for an exciting collection of art.

UNITED ARAB EMIRATES: Guests will immediately pass two ancient Arabic Dhows (sailing ships). Inside the pavilion, visitors first experience the excitement of a re-created Bedouin encampment. Located at the center of this deserted oasis will be the traditional ascetic black tents that symbolize Arabian warmth and hospitality. Then, guests are beckoned by the opulent royal marquis to enter an Arabian Nights experience, a thrilling magic carpet ride through the Arab World's most fascinating cultures, both past and present. As guests glide above the courtyard area, a powerful mythical character (a genie) appears before them to serve as narrator and guide through the adventure.

MOROCCO: At the end of a short journey over the promenade, an adventure into the life and personality of Morocco begins. The visitor may rest or photograph near the rustic paths and exotic plants of Hesperides Gardens before visiting the jagged rock formations of Hercules Grotto. An arcaded bridge with ceiling artwork depicting Morocco's five Great Dynasties connects the upper level of the grotto and Jemas Square.

Jemas Square is the gateway to the main body of the pavilion. The Koutoubia Minaret stands above the square, centerpieced by an elaborately decorated fountain, and from here glimpses of the Medina (ancient city) can be seen through the Bab Boujeloud Gate. The Medina opens into the Southern Morocco sector. Here, lunch can be enjoyed in a desert Kasbah where scenes of the Moroccan landscapes pass before the diners. Later in the evening, the Kasbah features a *Magic of Morocco* dinner show.

UNITED STATES: It was not actually considered part of the World Showcase but a massive glass and steel circular structure that sat on ultramodern stilts just across the bridge from Future World at the entrance where two merchandise shops are today.

It was designed to match the architectural theming of Future World and serve as a transition to the World Showcase. The pavilion was to be the "host" and when guests walked underneath the building (since the American Adventure show would be on the second floor) and left the United States, they would go to either Mexico or Canada, the two countries that bordered the U.S.

SPAIN: Take a spectacular journey through Spain by film to little-known and out-of-the-way vacation Edens. A ride attraction captures the country's passionate heritage and spirit in her arts. In a waterside restaurant indulge in tapas, or Spanish style finger food—a blend of varied ingredients but suitable to simple tastes. And browse the market places of striking contrast, from pueblo village to aristocratic opulence.

COSTA RICA: The architecture would have been Spanish colonial with a crystal palace containing a sample of the tropical gardens of Costa Rica featuring an orchid show at the entrance. The conservatory would cover nearly a third of an acre with beautiful flora, waterfalls, and tropical birds to create a very relaxing atmosphere. Outside would be a snack bar serving seafood and melons. Leather items, carved wood and similar items would be sold in the craft and merchandise area.

Imagineering created an impressive model for the pavilion and a Disney team brought it with them to the Costa Rican government for the final presentation. Unfortunately, the instability of the government prevented Disney from getting the firm commitments they needed from sponsors.

One of the most unique things about the Costa Rica pavilion was that the incredibly detailed model mysteriously disappeared soon after the presentation, prompting an extensive investigation by Imagineering. It was never recovered.

Imagineer David Mumford claimd:

> The model was one of the best we've ever built. It was insured so we recovered the money, but I think we lost a real treasure."

VENEZUELA: I interviewed Imagineer Alan Coats about the pavilion in 2012:

> I jump started development on the Venezuela pavilion with initial research on the country. Negotiation had been on going with several nations and the feeling was that it was a priority to include at least one country from the southern hemisphere. Brazil and Venezuela had shown interest in World Showcase participation.
>
> Using the WED research library, I assembled a series of storyboards, actually more like 'subject boards' on the history, culture, architecture, natural resources, festivals, whatever I could come up with as sort of a snapshot of the country. The overall idea for all the Showcase pavilions was to give the visitor a feeling of hav-

ing been to the country, if only briefly, to taste the food, listen to the music, purchase the merchandise, and meet some of the young people from the nation who would be working there.

These subject boards became the basis for renderings, models, and ride-system layouts that would follow. My dad [Claude Coats] as show designer used every foot available. He laid out a suspended cable-car ride that snaked through the attraction giving visitors a bird's eye view of activity below in the village sets filled with shops, the open restaurant, the musicians' stage, and other scenes. The entire area was dominated by a large-screen projection of Angel Falls in the background on a continuous film loop.

Collin Campbell painted a beautiful rendering of the interior in a nighttime setting. X. Atencio was show writer and also responsible for the theme song: *Discover Venezuela!* The show was really coming together when Gordon Cooper acknowledged in an interview with *Orlando-land* magazine in October 1976 that among ten or twelve pavilions in the works, full scale sections had been built and 'We're very far along on the Venezuela pavilion'. However, as we know, that nation never was represented in Showcase, nor was any other country in South America.

DENMARK: As early as 1979, the Disney Company was in discussions with the country of Denmark for a pavilion at World Showcase. At one time, it was intended to be located in an area between France and the United Kingdom and then when the waterway canal was proposed, the potential pavilion was moved to approximately where the Norway pavilion is today. As late as 1983, Disney was still in discussions with LEGO to help fund the pavilion.

Still hoping that the negotiations would be successful, Disney went ahead and built the outdoors bathrooms for the Danish pavilion to be available at the October 1982 opening, since the plan was that every other pavilion would have an easily accessible outdoor restroom (Norway, Germany, American Adventure, Morocco, United Kingdom) skipping the pavilions in between (Mexico, China, Italy, Japan, France, Canada) that would only have restrooms in the restaurants.

In addition, it was necessary to have these bathrooms in the empty area open and operating, especially since the plumbing infrastructure was in place and it would be more expensive later to incorporate it. Those restrooms blended in easily when the area was transformed into a Norway pavilion.

In 1983, it was determined that the pavilion would be devoted not just to Denmark but to include Sweden and Norway and would open in 1987. Egeskov Castle and some houses from Odense and Copenhagen would symbolize Denmark, while Sweden would be represented with Stockholm Stadshus and buildings from the Gamla Stan.

Right from the beginning, it was clear that the buildings representing Norway were going to be the Bryggen i Bergen and Akershus Festning, and they were still prominent in the pavilion when it finally opened.

Norway was the only country able to obtain the necessary funding. Norway put up more than two-thirds of the construction cost for the pavilion with Disney picking up the tab for the rest or roughly one-third.

The Norway Pavilion was the 11th and final (so far) country added to Epcot's World Showcase. It had a "soft opening" on May 6, 1988.

Other countries were in discussions for pavilions at the World Showcase including Russia (with a re-creation of Red Square), Iran (when the Shah was in power), and Switzerland (with a Matterhorn and the bobsled attraction).

Lafitte's Island (1998)

Eddie Sotto is a former Imagineer who worked for thirteen years at Disney. He remains one of the top designers and mixed-media producers in the world and is the founder in 2004 of Sotto Studios.

He also worked on projects for Universal Studios Hollywood, Knott's Berry Farm, and Six Flags, as well as countless other businesses.

Over the decades, Sotto has been very gracious and generous in sharing stories of his time working in Imagineering with the Disney fan community and that kindness was demonstrated again when I interviewed him in June 2018 about his plans for New Orleans Square at Disneyland.

Jim Korkis: How were you assigned to rehabbing the New Orleans Square area?

Eddie Sotto: There was tremendous pressure within the company to achieve 20% growth every year and to cut expenses. It was a very austere environment that we were working in. The management of Disneyland was under extreme pressure from corporate. I was at the top of the show master planning team down there under Tony Baxter.

Ops (Operations) philosophy was that we had been adding attractions over the years adding operating cost, and what we really needed to do was take something away if something was added.

High cost per guest carried was also an issue when it came to attractions like the Submarine Voyage, for example, as it was a very expensive attraction to operate (as is Indiana Jones and the Temple of the Forbidden Eye). Cuts had to made somewhere. Skyway closed during this period, partially for operating costs reasons.

The Tom Sawyer Island (TSI) rafts were under discussion as well. TSI needed upgrades to address aging assets and modern codes. Tony liked to re-imagine versus just replace the same assets when it came to rehabs (i.e. Tarzan's Treehouse). I felt the park needed balance in the "history driven" IP area versus everything being character driven. It was weakening the believability of the more historic areas like NOS.

JK: What did you think of Tom Sawyer's Island?

ES: Amazing. Growing up in a La Mirada tract house, it was the closest thing to a real adventure. Used to play "hide and seek" with friends there. The Fort fascinated me as it did most of my generation. *F Troop* was the hot TV show back then, so it was cool.

JK: Did the architecture of New Orleans Square inspire you as a kid?

ES: Very much so, still does. It's still my favorite land, like a backlot movie set. A masterpiece. My first serious book was *New Orleans and Its Environs: The Domestic Architecture 1727–1870*, a collection of historic images and measured drawings of the details.

As a ten year old, I would sit and copy the facades and draw the details all day. Then you'd compare the real to the land and connect the pieces the art directors used to make the land, a tower from this and a railing from that. Captivating. It was also restrained in its design, the colors were sophisticated. Romantic versus cute. Stunning that the interiors and merchandise so closely mirrored the theme! Cookery, Perfume, Antiques, Silver, etc.

This is the one land that when you went inside of the shops the theme got more powerful, versus diluted. Even the Rogues Gallery arcade had custom games! New Orleans Square was the benchmark for Main Street in Disneyland Paris as to the level of detail and research behind everything we did. I wanted to do something that rivaled that area of the park in quality and immersion.

JK: I understand you first started thinking of adding a more immersive pirate story to the area when you were in a grass hut in Hawaii?

ES: We were on vacation there in a literal hut on the beach. Thematically immersive! What better place to dream of Tall Ships, listening to the Norman Luboff *Songs of the Sea* (that plays on the Columbia Sailing Ship at Disneyland).

JK: Your ideas seemed to have emphasized the notorious pirate and privateer Jean Lafitte.

ES: I was looking for a connection to the Pirates attraction to do some sort of a pirate themed island idea. To even discuss it, we'd need to make it more profitable overall. I remember as a kid seeing the sign on the landing (in the Pirates of the Caribbean attraction) and that it was dedicated to Jean Lafitte. I purchased the highly disputed memoirs of the famed privateer and read them thoroughly and used that as the basis for the whole thing.

You also have the anchor along the Rivers of America that is jokingly dedicated to him as well. So it seemed like there were elements that already connected him. His connection to American history and actually being a patriot (very Disney) distanced him from the issue I had with glamorizing crime without consequence.

The discovery of an historic island adjacent to the real city of New Orleans that was used as a thieves market for the wealthy, emboldened me to the idea of making this a pirate driven island experience. You could never use the word Barratarria, but you could call it Lafitte's island or Pirate's Island, something like that. I felt a bit hesitant because making the whole island pirate themed doesn't resonate as well, with so many of the western elements on the Rivers of America.

As history has it, Lafitte was allegedly captured in Galveston Bay, Texas, so this particular theme historically does work. Still, this would have to be somewhat of a visually subtle transition, burying the pirate hideout under trees and earth. There would be no exposed pirate elements that the public can see because then it would never be a hideout!

Thematically speaking, the premise was to consider the south end of the island to be part of New Orleans Square as it faces the haunted mansion all the way down to the river boat landing.

As to books for research, the earliest one considered to being least sensational was *A Pirates' Own Book*. They were great stories of pirates from other countries and this inspired a few of the activities and other elements to the project.

I was very influenced by the Catacombs of Paris. They are filled with bones and are almost sculptural in nature and are extremely interesting to look at. I thought that creating a tunnel with continuous flow to and from the island would increase its potential from a business standpoint, help it operationally, and create an exciting way for a guest to experience the story as a pre-show.

I like the idea that the entire family experiences this mysterious title and an exciting show even before they get to the island. Most of the time, the parents sit on the bench while the kids run around for a half hour and it's not that exciting for everyone. This seemed like a big plus and the park is always been about exciting ways to get somewhere.

JK: Eventually, Disneyland did re-theme the island to Pirate's Lair.

ES: The fans have really driven the meta theme idea in a way that I never could. They've expanded far beyond where I had begun, and I guess that's a great thing. In the signage and story the Lafitte legend is woven in a bit too. The caves are well done with all kinds of interesting activities so again, that's all good. I probably would have not exposed so many large pirate elements outdoors, but that's a matter of opinion not right or wrong.

JK: I loved your idea of connecting New Orleans Square, Haunted Mansion and Tom Sawyer Island together using Jean Lafitte. Guests would discover a small cemetery near the Haunted Mansion. Among the headstones was a crypt for the Lafitte family and thieves have broken into it in search of pirate treasure. This would be the entrance to the secret underground passage going under the Rivers of America to Tom Sawyer Island where there would be a capsized series of scuttled ships hulls covered in earth as secret interior rooms and hideouts like a Pirates' Court and a Treasure Lair. What challenges would have confronted you with digging under the river and making it accessible for all guests?

ES: We never got that far. Things like digging a tunnel under the river is far more of a topic of concern than any kind of thematic aberration. I don't think I really got any pushback except from Paul Pressler who reviewed it in a very short meeting, turned it down, and that was it.

Tony I think really liked idea though and it seemed to be part of a larger series of ideas that was presented. I don't think the idea got much play. Certainly Jack Sparrow crowing about all the redeeming qualities of a life of crime at the end of Pirates of the Caribbean with no consequence at all certainly trumps any kind of social conscience they might've had about that.

JK: Who else was involved in this project?

ES: This was pretty much something small that I cooked up on my own on vacation and brought back to the team. Matt McKim worked on the Fantasmic! upgrade project (terracing the riverfront for viewing) and our show quality team.

It's his date of birth (minus two hundred years) that happens to be over the bricked-in arch that has been the subject of such discussion over the years. He was assisting in the carving of the stone at the time. Matt is a great guy by the way and the son of the legendary Imagineer Sam McKim.

That whole waterfront upgrade was inspired by a place I visited years earlier in Savannah, Georgia called Factors Walk. Stone ballast was brought in from English ships, offloaded and then turned into the Cobblestone and retaining walls. Cotton replaced the ballast as export.

I wanted to show that the waterfront had lived more than one life and had layers of theme, as Europe does. I thought the arch that was bricked-in would be a great way of showing that something was there at one time, but later removed or sealed.

JK: Would there have been plaques explaining things to guests?

ES: Yes, in Lafitte's Catacomb, you'd have plaques you could make rubbings from with clues, etc. I think plaques are great as we have annual passholders now who are always searching to drill deeper into the story. I would rather just have strong visuals, like the tomb of Lafitte decorated in cannons with dedication plaques to each crew and each ship that was sacked. You would hear perhaps sound effects and things that would tell the story. In a perfect world, a kid would want to research more about the real stories of these real people.

JK: How would you have handled guests with disabilities?

ES: I imagine there would be a second crypt that would actually be an elevator that would connect to the tunnel on either end. There is not enough land to do ramping.

JK: What would have been removed from the island?

ES: We would probably have re-imagined all of the cave experiences and take out the fort. An earth structure, almost like a berm with trees and gun ports would be coming out of the sod; inside, it's a capsized ship hideout. I always enjoyed the scenes in the film *Goonies* where the kids end up in this Pirates Lair. What kid would not enjoy doing that?

JK: I was told that you considered some details like a cannon-firing arcade and a saloon where you could get pop-rocks mixed in your drinks in imitation of Chinese pirates, who mixed gunpowder in their grog. Would there have been references to Disney films like *Treasure Island*?

ES: If we would've actually had a budget to go further, I'm sure there would've been a lot of elements from all of those films. The small details you don't wait in line for that just make Disneyland more believable are very valuable and precious to me. That's why the upstairs window sound effects on Main Street came back or the laughing apple at Snow White. Most people enjoy those little details that could only happen at Disneyland.

JK: How was Lafitte to tie in with the Haunted Mansion?

ES: That's something fans created because some of the leftover props that involved Andrew Jackson (in Fort Wilderness on the island), and they got recycled in the Haunted Mansion. The mansion is a part of the river front of New Orleans, so to me it just naturally fit in. Lafitte being in the common graveyard across from it seemed like a natural tie-in without getting too literal about it.

JK: Why did you move Lafitte's anchor to where it is today?

ES: I was on vacation first in Hawaii and thinking things through second. The anchor was most likely subconscious and when it came to re-doing the waterfront we decided to make that a more central element as part of the show. I thought it was more appropriate in front of New Orleans Square than it was in front of the Golden Horseshoe.

JK: You left Imagineering in 1999. Did the fact that this project didn't go forward influence that decision?

ES: I guess you could say that. Overall, the appetite for doing new things and pushing the envelope is what drives me and if that appetite wasn't there or I don't see opportunity, then I feel like I have to reinvent myself in other ways and other places. It so happened that other opportunities such as the Internet and television came along when there was a bit of a hiatus creatively at WDI.

At that time, projects like Tokyo DisneySea and Euro Disneyland were not seen as the future. Disney California Adventure and Hong Kong Disneyland were the new direction. I did not really feel challenged by that as they were "lite" versions of the kinds of things I was used to doing.

I'm always excited by challenging, exciting projects. But the atmosphere set by management did not seem to be that challenging and so other opportunities caught my eye.

WDI has its "pendulum swings" and they are in a historically amazing period right now with so much going on. It's all about timing.

Liberty Street (1959)

Walt Disney felt that many Americans, especially children, failed to fully appreciate the significance of their patriotic heritage. In the early days of Disneyland, Walt was developing plans for an area to provide guests with a better understanding and a greater pride in the American way of life.

This area was to be called Liberty Street. Just to the left of the Disneyland Opera House would have been a street that would have paralleled Main Street.

However, you wouldn't have been able to take the street to the Hub. It was to be a cul-de-sac. Only Main Street would have given you the option to visit other lands.

Publicity and signage at Disneyland announced that this area was scheduled to open in 1959. Originally the street was going to be International Street and that was announced as opening in 1958 but Walt changed his mind because of the release of the live action Disney feature film, *Johnny Tremain* (originally intended as merely a two-part episode for the Disneyland television show) in 1957.

It certainly may have influenced Walt to consider the development of an area capturing that time period, especially since the first planning for Liberty Square began in 1957.

Walt's daughter, Sharon, had her one and only film role—a small one—in this film, although the Disney publicity machine certainly shone a lot of its light on her performance.

Liberty Street was to be an architectural mixture of several America cities as they existed during the Revolutionary War era. At one point there were to be thirteen buildings, one for each of the original 13 colonies. Cobblestones would pave the way down Liberty Street and into Liberty Square.

There would be a blacksmith shop, apothecary, glassmaker, weaver, print shop, insurance office, silversmith and cabinetmaker. All the shops and exhibits would represent the types of enterprises that might be found in Colonial America. In fact, the shops were supposed to showcase people not only selling their wares but also practicing their crafts for guests to enjoy.

The original outline for the project stated that "the audience will walk around the street toward Independence Hall where the Liberty

Bell would be constantly tolling." (Fortunately, in Florida, wiser heads realized a constantly tolling Liberty Bell would be more of an irritant than a joy when they installed their own replica of the Liberty Bell.)

One of the exhibits in Liberty Square would be a scale model of the Capitol building. (Long-time Disneyland visitors might remember it used to be displayed for many years at Disneyland in the pre-show area of The Walt Disney Story.) The model was personally purchased by Walt Disney himself from an artisan who had devoted twenty-five years of his life to carving it out of stone.

Liberty Hall (also called Independence Hall in some versions) was the centerpiece of the Liberty Square and was the entrance to the two major attractions in this land: Hall of The Declaration of Independence, and Hall of Presidents of the United States. A large foyer with dioramas depicting famous scenes of the Revolutionary War period would be the common entrance to the two big auditoriums.

The Hall of The Declaration of Independence was designed to present the dramatic story of the birth of the United States through three scenes that were based on three famous paintings.

These scenes would be three framed settings with three-dimensional sculpted life-sized human figures in costume. It was hoped the figures would move realistically but in a limited fashion. Narration (sprinkled with quotes from the Declaration) would tell the story and historical significance of each tableau along with dramatic lighting and music. Theatrical curtains would open and close on each scene.

The first scene was inspired by the painting "The Drafting of the Declaration of Independence" by J.L.G. Ferris. The scene has Ben Franklin and John Adams in consultation with Thomas Jefferson as he drafted the Declaration of Independence.

The second scene would be based on the painting "Signing of the Declaration of Independence" by John Trumbull. The third scene would be based on the painting "Ringing of the Liberty Bell" by Henry Mosler.

Of course, the theater would try to capture the feel of the time period. There would be bench-like pews that could seat up to 500 guests. Overhead, 13 stars representing the original thirteen colonies would light the auditorium.

In The Hall of Presidents of the United States auditorium, the stage lights would brighten and the curtains would partially open to reveal life-sized sculpted and costumed figures of the presidents of the United States. They would all be in silhouette except for the main figure. The key U.S. president would not have been Lincoln but George Washington.

The show was entitled *One Nation Under God* and would be a theater presentation of "the mighty cavalcade of American History".

Imagineer David Mumford several decades ago in an article on "Lost Disneyland" for *WDEye*, the in-house magazine for Walt Disney Imagineering, wrote:

> Martial music would come up as lights played on the features of Washington, creating a feeling of reality. Narrations of the trials, decisions and formation of America's heritage were to be complemented by excerpts from presidential speeches. At the conclusion, all the nation's presidents (34 by 1957) would be seen on the enormous stage against a rear-projected image of the United States Capitol, as clouds panned across the sky and a musical finale closed the show.

Obviously, this show would depend heavily on the development of audio-animatronics which was still in its earliest of stages. WED had begun producing prototypes, including the head of an elderly Chinese man for a figure that Walt had originally intended for a Chinese restaurant that would have been in Center Street near the Market House. An elderly Chinese man reminiscent of Confucius wearing long flowing robes would have justified any shaky, slow, awkward movements when the figure moved.

WED was working on a prototype of President Lincoln, a particular favorite of Walt's, for the Hall of Presidents attraction when Robert Moses who was promoting the New York World's Fair dropped by the Disney Studios and got a demonstration of the figure. Moses arranged for the State of Illinois to help pay for the development of the figure for its pavilion at the fair. Although crude by today's standards, the "winking, blinking Lincoln" thrilled audiences. Many were convinced it was a live actor.

A second version of Great Moments With Mr. Lincoln was installed at Disneyland on July 18, 1965, mere feet away from where the entrance to Liberty Street was planned.

Instead of creating Liberty Street in 1959, Walt Disney used his money and expertise to update Tomorrowland with the Monorail, the Submarine Voyage and the Matterhorn.

However, Imagineering never fully abandoned Walt's dream. Walt Disney World's Liberty Square captures the spirit of Walt's plans for Disneyland in 1959 including a Hall of Presidents. In fact, the script and some of the actual recordings in the original version of the show that opened in 1971 were done under Walt's personal supervision for the Disneyland Liberty Street project around 1960.

Edison Square (1959)

Inspired by Walt Disney's memories of Marceline, Missouri (as well some memories of Imagineer Harper Goff's boyhood in Fort Collins, Colorado), Main Street, U.S.A. at Disneyland Park is a small but prosperous, rural Midwestern city at the turn-of-the-century.

Early in the planning, Walt had wanted a side street extension at the end of Main Street with such familiar landmarks as a schoolhouse, a church, and a haunted house. Time and limited finances did not allow for it, but as Disneyland became a huge success in its first few years, Walt once again considered using that area for a future expansion.

At the end of Main Street, on the right side of the Hub, would have been another more urban, residential street called Edison Square. It would have been built on what was then known as "Plaza Street" near the Plaza Inn (at that time called the Red Wagon Inn). It was announced that Edison Square would open Easter 1959.

As shown in a full-color concept painting by Imagineer Sam McKim, the entrance to this suburban addition would resemble a gated community with two red brick pillars supporting a curved all electric sign saying "Edison Square."

There would be a brick paved street, the most modern of electric and gas-powered "horseless carriages" and, of course, "brand new" electric street lights instead of Main Street's gas lamps.

The facades of the buildings would recall the red brick houses of Philadelphia, New York's brownstones, the wooden edifices of St. Louis and San Francisco, the graystones of Chicago, and the colonial brick of Boston—truly making it part of a larger Main Street U.S.A., rather than just a small Midwestern town.

Prominently displayed at the center of this cul-de-sac area in a little fenced-in circular, green park would have been a life-sized statue of inventor Thomas Edison, with his right arm raised high in the air and his finger pointing upward.

From the 1958 Disney proposal to General Electric:

> Edison Square in Disneyland will dramatically present the story of the way in which one invention by Thomas A. Edison has influenced the growth and development of America. ... Edison Square is the story of that era: the birth, growth, development and future of electricity and General Electric products.

> Located just a few steps from Main Street, Edison Square will be the passing of the "old" of the 19th century to the "new" of the 1900s. As they [the guests] enter Progress Place in Edison Square, where they will find that "Progress Is Our Most Important Product," visitors will see two separate plaques on which General Electric's symbol and appropriate words setting forth the theme of Edison Square will appear.
>
> Inside the buildings, General Electric's theatrical productions will be staged for Disneyland visitors. Edison Square will be alive and vital. Disneyland's "horseless carriages" and surreys which travel up and down Main Street will move in and out of the area. Such annual Disneyland special events as the "Horseless Carriage Day Parade" and the "Easter Parade" will be a part of Edison Square.
>
> The square itself will be architecturally landscaped befitting the turn-of-the-century. It will contain the "new" electric lamps, iron grill work, hitching posts and other "signs of the times." All the windows in the buildings will be authentically dressed and specially lighted to carry out the atmosphere of the area.

Walt Disney had quickly learned that major corporations partnering on a Disneyland attraction could be beneficial to everyone. Walt got funding for research and development of his concepts that could not only be used in the attraction itself but also expanded in other areas.

The companies got an important "billboard" showcase where their name and products were tied to happiness and magic and had a captive, receptive audience. Walt was clever to promote projects that not only met the needs of the client but also the guests and the Disney organization.

One of the early successes was the Circarama attraction in Tomorrowland sponsored by American Motors. American Motors Corporation (AMC) was an American automobile company formed on January 14, 1954, by the merger of the Nash-Kelvinator Corporation and the Hudson Motor Car Company.

On the floor inside the attraction were prominently displayed five AMC automobiles, as well as Kelvinator appliances. These appliances included the futuristic "Foodarama" refrigerator. As a result, Imagineering Legend Dick Irvine called these types of projects "refrigerator shows" where the product had to be incorporated in the most positive way into the show.

After the opening of Disneyland Park, General Electric's Lamp Division had visited Walt at WED to discuss the possibilities of sponsoring an attraction at Disneyland. While they were clear about what they wanted to advertise, they left it to Walt's storytelling to come up with an appropriate showcase.

The result was a new area for the park spotlighting a unique four-act play with a prologue and epilogue entitled *Harnessing the Lightning*. Imagineer John Hench recalled:

> [This project] was inspired by Thornton Wilder's *Our Town*. But we changed it all, because the original play had no sets, just bare stage, a brick wall at the back of the theater in New York.... It was really quite a touching play. I saw it three times, I think. I came back and told Walt I thought that's what we should do for General Electric.

Walt saw *Our Town* at least three times when it was performed in Los Angeles and also enjoyed the play.

Our Town is a three-act theatrical play written by American playwright Thornton Wilder. On a simple stage with minimal props and using a stage manager as a narrator, it tells the story of George Gibbs and Emily Webb and their daily lives in the small town of Grover's Corners, New Hampshire, in a selection of scenes from 1901 to 1913.

Harnessing the Lightning would be performed in a hidden horseshoe theater with multiple stages inside the buildings at the far end of the cul-de-sac of Edison Square. In four acts, it would follow a typical American family through the decades with each step showing how GE had made the future brighter and better.

Mr. Wilbur K. Watt, the "K" standing for "Kilo," would be the on stage narrator for the show.

According to the brochure prepared for GE: "Our narrator, Wilbur K. Watt, is an incredible electro-mechanical man. As he rocks back and forth in his armchair, he describes the scene we see on stage. It is almost as though Mr. Watt were alive, for his movements are synchronized and life-like as he describes the play."

Once again, Sam McKim did a detailed sketch of the exterior of the show buildings with Imagineer Herb Ryman doing a more detailed rendering of the interior stages over McKim's concept drawing of what the entire area would look like.

The show would cover more than 40,000 square feet of lobby, theaters and GE product display area. Walt was always very keenly aware of audience control.

The plan was to have a lobby with five animated dioramas (like those proposed for the Liberty Street shows) to corral no more than 125 people. The overly generous estimate was that 2,125 guests per hour would be able to enjoy the show. This area would be the prologue to the show.

At the appropriate time, doors would open in front of them and this group of no more than 125 people would be funneled into the first theater. The audience would stand on a four-tiered platform with each tier separated by continuous railing very similar to the pre-show of Stitch's Great Escape attraction today.

When the scene was finished on the first stage, the lights would dim and automatic doors would open to allow guests to move into the next area to see the next scene while another group was funneled in behind them to see the first act.

There were a total of four acts lasting a total of fifteen minutes. After the final act, the guests would enter an epilogue room showcasing GE products.

The playbill for the show, done in appropriate lettering and silhouetted pointing hands and other flourishes, stated: "General Electric presents Edison Square, Disneyland U.S.A. An astounding dramatization. 'Harnessing the Lightning.' A story of Yesterday, Today and Tomorrow. A feast for eye and ear in four great acts with prologue and epilogue. Mr. Wilbur K. Watt. The Incredible Electric Man supported by a most amazing cast of 50 marvelous electro-mechanical personalities that sing, dance, and talk."

Dance? That might have been hyperbole or wishful thinking on Walt's part, or maybe even a fond memory of his previous little dancing man project. Audio-Animatronics had yet to be developed. "Electromechanicals" were the type of simple figures with limited repetitive movements like the friendly Indian chief lifting his arm on the shores of the Rivers of America or the unfriendly natives at the end of the Jungle Cruise. Basically, electricity controlled a simple mechanical movement cycle like a hippo wiggling its ears or surfacing.

However, Walt hoped with strong storytelling, dramatic lighting, further technological developments and limited time for each act (roughly three minutes) that it might be effective. In addition, Hench had suggested that the figures be "highly stylized" so that they didn't resemble a realistic human being too closely.

They would have more caricatured bodies and oval shaped heads so that if they didn't move smoothly or made a jumpy action, it would still be accepted by the audience. They were not cartoons, nor were they human but some intermediate hybrid.

What would the show have been like?

PROLOGUE: "THE WIZARD'S PROGRESS." The room would have four full dimensional dioramas spotlighting achievements in the life of Edison. There would be a smaller side room gallery for the final fifth diorama titled "40 Hour Watch" showing Edison and his associates achieving their goal in 1879 of an incandescent lamp that burned for 40 consecutive hours. This was the finale and led into the first theater.

ACT I. 1898. "1% Inspiration—99% Perspiration." The days before electricity in a typical American home. Sitting in a rocking chair is Wilbur K. Watt . The characters demonstrate the newest home appliances like the washing machine, a new stove, an ice box and even a phonograph. Basically, most household marvels are human powered.

ACT II. 1918. POST WAR. "The Initials of a Friend." *(The initials, by the way, are G.E.)* Although he is not named, Cousin Orville in the bathtub with his own version of "air cooling" made an appearance. There is still the jungle of wires to run the new devices like household lighting, refrigeration, toasters, water heaters and other applicances. Watt points out how thankful we all are for that new company founded by Tom Edison, General Electric.

ACT III. 1958. "Live Better Electrically." John Hench came up with the idea of having the children wearing Mickey Mouse ears sitting on the floor watching the Mickey Mouse Club on a small black and white television. Remember at the time, this was the present. So it was the interior of an upscale contemporary home where mom and dad enjoy modern comforts like climate controlled radiant heat, television, "hot food from a cold oven" and "a poached egg in 20 seconds!"

ACT IV. 19?8. The question mark in the date is intentional since this was some undetermined time in the future. "More Power to America." A penthouse overlooking New York City. It is an Electronic Island in the Sky with stars both above and below. Predicted products included space scanners, luminous walls, self propelled serving carts, protein measurements, programmer controlled kitchen (a prototype of a personal computer), microwave oven, and other new, automatic time-saving devices.

Guests would have been invited to actually step on stage to experience the home of the future...but only within the three-minute time limit. At the close of the act, the interplanetary large screen television showed Wilbur K. Watt landing on the planet Venus in a rocket ship with a GE logo. "We step confidently into the future," he assured us.

EPILOGUE: "Progress is Our Most Important Product." This room was called the General Electric Institutional Product Room where G.E. could promote both its existing products and those coming soon.It was the equivalent of a Disneyland attraction exiting into a gift shop.

Walt was enthusiastic about the project. It incorporated his beliefs in the importance of the American family and how the future and the technological progress it would bring was something to be embraced.

Edison Square appeared on the 1958 Disneyland park map and remained there up to 1964. McKim's sketch of the entrance to Edison

Square appeared in the 1959 Disneyland Guidebook, as well. It was obvious that this new area would be opening soon.

A brochure was prepared for General Electric with artwork by Sam McKim, Herb Ryman and Paul Hartley (who was in charge of the graphics department) in two colors on good stock paper.

United States Justice Department indicted General Electric for price fixing on electrical equipment. GE's fine was almost $500,000, with an additional $50 million in damages paid to utilities who had purchased price-fixed equipment. Three GE managers received jail sentences and several others were forced to leave the company.

GE hoped to improve their image with an impressive pavilion at the forthcoming 1964 World's Fair. What better way to clean up a public image than by partnering with the much-beloved Walt Disney whose name stood for quality and integrity?

Walt suggested utilizing the Edison Square proposal, but with an innovative new theater that would drastically increase capacity and the development of Audio-Animatronics that would provide greater entertainment value.

With some script revisions, the show became: The Carousel Theater Show, and then was changed to The Carousel Theater of Progress and finally just The Carousel of Progress. The similarities in style and content between the two shows are very obvious.

At the World's Fair, an average of 41,000 visitors saw the show every day. By the end of the fair, more than 16 million people had seen the attraction. Surveys conducted by General Electric revealed that 87 percent of the audience rated the show as "excellent" and 12 percent as "good."

People gladly waited in line (under blue and white canopied covered queue lines) for 90 minutes to view the show. From Edison Square to The Carousel of Progress. ... Now, *that's* progress!

Thunder Mesa (1975)

Despite its popularity, the Pirates of the Caribbean originally was not considered to be added to the new Magic Kingdom in Florida.

Imagineer Tony Baxter said:

> For some reason, it was thought that because of Florida's close proximity to the Caribbean, a ride dealing with pirates wouldn't be as popular in Walt Disney World as it was in Disneyland.

Disney determined that the Florida coast and surrounding vicinity had been home to real pirates and there were many locations and museums devoted to them so guests would not be interested in visiting an artificial experience. In addition, it was discussed that the attraction might actually be considered disrespectful of the true history of pirates by the Florida residents.

However, Disney failed to take into account that the Pirates of the Caribbean attraction did not deal with real pirates but with the mythology of pirates reflected in books and movies.

In addition, east coast guests had heard and seen so much about the iconic Disneyland attraction that they eagerly wanted an opportunity to experience it without having to travel to the west coast.

The Imagineers also wanted some attractions that were exclusive to WDW and not just a duplication of Disneyland. The intention was that there were some attractions that could only be enjoyed at Disneyland and others that could only be enjoyed at Walt Disney World.

Creating a similar attraction using everything they had learned seemed to be the perfect solution. Turning to Imagineer Marc Davis who had been the main designer of POtC for that similar alternative, Davis came up with an entire area to be located at the edge of WDW's Frontierland to be called Thunder Mesa. It was felt that a Wild West experience would be something out-of-the-ordinary for east coast guests.

However, Davis did not plan just a simple attraction that would be humorous and menacing like POtC but an entire new land that would be connected to Frontierland in general theme yet still be its own separate area.

Thunder Mesa would have been a massive mountain that featured a variety of attractions including the Western River Expedition, a runaway mine train roller coaster ride to be called Thunder Railway, hiking trails past natural arches, waterfalls, desert flora and fauna and pack mule riding trails on the upper bluff, a Pueblo Native American village and more including a Western town called Mesa Terrace that would have featured a themed restaurant.

To accommodate all of this, a four story show building would have been built and decorated to look like the orange mesas of the American desert and, in particular, Utah's Monument Valley. The WDW railroad would have gone directly through the building to offer guests a glimpse of some of these adventures and to excite them about visiting.

The new mesa would have been approximately in the space Splash Mountain and Big Thunder Mountain now occupy at WDW. Acreage had been cleared for it in early 1971.

The Walt Disney World Preview Edition from 1970 states: "Thunder Mesa will tower high above dense pine forests, offering a spectacular panoramic view of Frontierland."

The Western River Expedition attraction was the crown jewel of this new extension to Frontierland.

It was jokingly referred to by Imagineers as "Cowboys of the Caribbean" because of its superficial similarities to the Pirates of the Caribbean attraction at Disneyland in terms of its design and experiences. It was a boat ride with waterfalls, humorous scenes, a theme song, and dozens of audio-animatronics characters designed by Marc Davis.

However, closer inspection shows that it would have been much more technologically advanced and complex as well as the fact that the music would be more closely integrated with the story of the ride.

Davis spent five years creating a humorous ten to twelve minute boat trip through a variety of Wild West scenes. It was based on a concept he had developed as early as 1963 about a Lewis and Clark River Expedition for the never built St. Louis Riverfront Square indoor theme park Walt Disney was considering.

The Western River Shipping & Navigation Company was the home to the Western River Expedition.

Guests would have entered through a mine shaft tunnel decorated with oversized covers of Dime Novels featuring characters like Davy Crockett and Annie Oakley and deeper into the mountain would have boarded boats.

Those vehicles would have taken them onto a winding river through a cave with "perpetual twilight lighting" where the stalactites and stalagmites eerily resembled old West characters both human and animal. It was very similar to the cave transition that occurs in POtC.

Scenes in the attraction would have featured:

- A group of threatening stagecoach robbers (where even the horses they rode wore bandana masks to hide their identity). The leader, a singing bandit, warns that they will meet the guests again further down the river.

- An open prairie with prairie dogs, antelopes, buffaloes, singing cowboys and singing cacti.

- The town of Dry Gulch on a raucous Saturday night with can-can dancing saloon girls, a drunken cowboy on horseback on top of the saloon porch roof, prisoners escaping from the jail under the nose of an unsuspecting sheriff, hooting and hollering cowboys, and other characters.

- A desert where comic Native American figures performed a rain dance with disastrous results. For comedic effect, these figures would have been exaggerated stereotypes similar to the cartoon Indians in Disney films like *The Saga of Windwagon Smith* (1961) and *Peter Pan* (1953).

Guests would then go up a waterfall into a forest where trees had been set ablaze by the lightning storm created in the earlier rain scene. To make matters worse, the bandits from earlier have indeed caught up with the boats and seek to do harm but the guests escape down a waterfall and through another cave to arrive back at the boarding area of the attraction.

It would have contained approximately a hundred and fifty audio-animatronics figures. A buffalo and prairie dogs were actually built for the attraction and later incorporated into the opening ranch house scene in the Living with the Land attraction at Epcot.

Davis spent many long months working on the attraction and had the enthusiastic support of both Roy O. Disney and President of Imagineering Dick Irvine when he started the project. As the years progressed, both of these key champions passed away.

Detailed sketches were made and models were created. Imagineer Mitsou Natsume even built a detailed model of Thunder Mesa and the exterior of the Western River Shipping & Navigation Company.

The saloon scene with the cowboy on the roof was displayed from April 1973 until the spring of 1981 in the post-show area of The Walt Disney Story on Main Street USA at the Magic Kingdom. It was scaled one inch to the foot and the figures were sculpted by Ken O'Brien.

The background music was a one minute loop of the honky-tonk piano version of *The Merrily Song* that also played in Mr. Winky's Pub in the Mr. Toad's Wild Ride attraction in Fantasyland.

An audio-animatronics owl named Hoot Gibson sat nearby on a tree branch perch and when a guest pressed a button, he would spring to life to talk about audio-animatronics and promote the upcoming Thunder Mesa.

Hoot Gibson was a silent movie cowboy and so the name was not only a reference to the mythology of the Wild West but a reference to the fact that owls hoot.

Gibson voiced by actor Junius Matthews said, "Who am I? Why, hee hee, I'm the real Hoot Gibson, that's who. I'm the star of a brand new western show being made for Walt Disney World. I sure hope you'll come back and see me in the future at the Western River Expedition right here in Walt Disney World."

The owl was designed by Davis to give the safety spiel for guests boarding the boats and perhaps to act as a host in the rest of the attraction making comical remarks.

At one point, color stylist Mary Blair, a good friend of Davis and his wife, was brought in to consult with the color choices including a Painted Desert backdrop. She ended up producing a large amount of concept art to help illustrate the story.

Composer Buddy Baker had the beginnings of a theme song that would repeat throughout the ride in different musical styles to match the different scenes.

The attraction was publicized with concept art in the Magic Kingdom guidebooks for 1971 and 1972 since the project was supposed to open with the park but because of time and budget factors was relegated to Phase 2 that would be completed by 1975.

It made no sense to tackle the massive construction challenges of Thunder Mesa when all resources were being diverted to opening WDW by October 1971 so the challenging project was postponed.

Many factors contributed to the eventual demise of Thunder Mesa including prohibitive costs (estimated conservatively at over a hundred and twenty million dollars), the decline in popularity of Western movies and TV shows, the energy crisis in the early 1970s that significantly cut back on visitors to the park and primarily, guests demanding a Pirates of the Caribbean attraction.

Disney president Card Walker put Thunder Mesa on temporary hiatus while resources and finances were directed to quickly building the Pirates of the Caribbean attraction that opened in 1973 because it would be a guaranteed success and drive additional attendance. In addition it cost less than half what Western River Expedition would cost. Davis worked on the new version.

Walker was always fiscally conservative and would have liked to cancel the entire Thunder Mesa project just to save the company some money. However, he hoped that WDW would be so financially successful that money could then be used for building Thunder Mesa and perhaps create a reason for guests to schedule future repeat trips much sooner than planned.

During this time, Davis pitched the idea of the Western River Expedition as a stand alone attraction as a possible replacement for the Mine Train Through Nature's Wonderland in Disneyland's Frontierland. In the mid-1970s, the "Disneyland Showcase" preview center at the front of the park actually featured a Western River Expedition model as well as some of Davis' concept paintings so obviously the idea was being seriously considered.

However, Walker had a different idea for that same area and decided to take part of the Thunder Mesa proposal, a runaway mine train thrill ride, and have Imagineer Tony Baxter adapt and expand it into a separate attraction to be called Big Thunder Mountain Railroad. It was decided that the word "mountain" rather than "mesa" would be more familiar to guests and "railroad" more familiar than "railway". He had been impressed by the young Imagineer's ideas to make the ride more thrilling and story-oriented when he reviewed the model.

Davis was incensed and held a grudge against Baxter for the rest of his life, feeling his project had been undercut. Davis was offered the opportunity to produce a scaled-down version of Western River Expedition to be placed side-by-side with the new runaway train attraction in a show building that would have had a rock facade.

Davis did do a smaller version that included removing the potentially offensive stereotypically comic Native Americans (often replacing them with Caucasian counterparts) and Walker asked as well for Davis to try to determine if already existing POtC audio-animatronics could be "re-skinned" for the attraction to further save money. Davis adamantly and vocally balked at that last suggestion.

Davis' official retirement in 1978 meant the loss of the attraction's still living biggest advocate and when ground breaking for the Big Thunder Mountain Railroad happened in 1979 at WDW on the land set aside for Thunder Mesa, it was apparent that the dream of Thunder Mesa was officially cancelled.

In addition, all available finances as well as all other resources at the time were being targeted to the opening of Epcot Center. Yet, Western River Expedition had become so legendary that it refused to disappear.

When Disneyland Paris opened in 1992, Frontierland's fictional town was named Thunder Mesa as a tribute to the Davis project. In 1993, Jeff Burke, show producer of Disneyland Paris' Frontierland considered building a version of Western River Expedition on the land available behind the train station. However, Disney CEO Michael Eisner thought it would be too expensive to pursue.

In 1994, the ghost of Thunder Mesa once more appeared. At Walt Disney World, when the post-show area of the Walt Disney Story was changed in 1981 to promote the upcoming Epcot Center, the elaborate display for the Western River Expedition model was not removed. Workmen simply covered up its glass display case with fiber board because it was cheaper and faster.

Thirteen years later when the area was changed again to promote WDW's 25th anniversary, a new workman pulled down the fiber board and discovered the forgotten display and found not only the model still intact but that the electricity had not been disconnected so all the tiny lights in the model were still lit.

When WDW Imagineers were notified they immediately came and took documentation photos and then carefully packed everything up and sent it to Walt Disney Imagineering in Glendale where it is now housed in its Research Library.

PART THREE

The Television Shows That Never Were

Walt told an interviewer:

> I saw that if I was ever going to have my [Disneyland] park here at last was a way to tell millions of people about it...with TV. TV was the start of Disneyland.

His deal with ABC also gave that network the first option on any other television shows that Walt Disney Productions would produce.

ABC ended up airing two other series produced by WDP, the original *Mickey Mouse Club* and *Zorro*. However, Walt became frustrated at how ABC handled both series and was upset when both were unceremoniously cancelled by the network.

Walt said to *TV Guide* writer Bill Davidson in 1961:

> When I came up with a fresh idea, the network executives would say "no." Just to give you some notion of what they turned down, one of their rejects was *The Shaggy Dog*. We made a theater movie out of it and it grossed nine million dollars.

Walt had pitched ABC the idea as a weekly series in 1958 but network executive Jim Aubrey expressed extreme disinterest. Infuriated, Walt turned it into one of the top grossing films of the year and it became a springboard for a series of Disney live action feature film comedies.

Harrison "Buzz" Price when he was researching the best possible place for Disneyland had to take into account a good location for television transmission because Walt intended to broadcast from the park. One of the restrictions on the Anaheim property was that obstructions such as power lines couldn't be in direct line from the park to the antennas atop Mount Wilson in the San Gabriel Mountains.

Originally, Walt had considered making Mickey Mouse Island in Frontierland with a hollow tree headquarters for the Mickey Mouse Club and broadcasting a live show each day featuring the Mouseketeers in different areas of Disneyland to promote the park.

In 1962, Disney did produce a local television show broadcast directly from Disneyland once a week on KTTV (Channel 11). Entitled *Meet Me At Disneyland,* it ran from June 1962 to September 1962 for thirteen episodes in an attempt to boost weeknight attendance at Disneyland during the summer months.

There were plans to build a television studio at Epcot Center "where we will have live audiences and be doing live television for cable," claimed executive Dick Nunis in an article in the October 24, 1982, edition of *The Orlando Sentinel.* "We don't have a date on it...but our top executives really want to go forward with it, so I'm sure we will do it."

Disney experimented with several limited television series from 1982 to 1985 like *Herbie, the Love Bug* and *Zorro and Son* but none of them did particularly well. It wasn't until the debut of the Disney Channel in 1983 and the purchase of the ABC network in 1996, that Disney aggressively produced original television series.

The following chapters share just a few of the many television shows that almost aired.

Jim Henson's
The Little Mermaid's Island (1990)

Music is everywhere! Music is in the air!
On Little Mermaid's Island, come ashore!
Far from the quiet of the ocean floor,
If music's what you're looking for,
Come on and play!

On Little Mermaid's Island, life is grand
Up where the waves caress the sand!
When you hear the Mermaid's Island band,
Come on and play!

That opening theme song was joyfully sung by a live-action Ariel the Little Mermaid and her crab friend Sebastian, a puppet created by Jim Henson's Creature Shop, in a television series that will never be seen.

Henson himself was a huge fan of Disney and flirted with the idea of merging with the Disney Company at least once or twice before a deal was put in process in late 1989 where Henson would sell his famous Muppet characters (minus the ones from Sesame Street) to the Walt Disney Company.

Henson was very tired of the business side and wanted to focus more on the creative side of things. Henson was certainly innovative and part of the deal was that the Disney Company would have exclusive use of Henson's creative services for ten years. Unfortunately, Henson died on May 16, 1990 after organ failure from an advanced infection of a rare bacterium that was discovered too late for him to receive proper treatment in the hospital.

With his death, the unsigned contract remained unsigned because of some things that needed to still be resolved. Negotiations with the Henson heirs finally fell apart by December 1990 and by 1991 several lawsuits and hard feelings were generated that took time to resolve.

However, it was clearly Henson's intent to sign the contract since he was already deeply involved in several Disney-related projects including the much loved Jim Henson's Muppet*Vision 3-D attraction at Disney Hollywood Studios and a television special of the Muppets visiting Walt Disney World.

In addition to other Disney Muppet-related projects from a parade to a live-action show to expanding an area of the Disney MGM Studios into a Muppet Studios land, Henson was working on several other projects, including a live-action *The Little Mermaid's Island* television series. Jim Henson passed away about two months after the pilot for that never seen half-hour show for the Disney Channel was shot.

The animated feature *The Little Mermaid* had been released in the fall of 1989 and was an immediate hit grossing more than $200 million dollars worldwide. When the film was released on home video in May 1990, it was one of the highest-selling home videos up to that time, including seven million units sold in the first month alone.

In the fall of 1992, an animated Saturday morning cartoon series of the adventures of a younger Ariel and her friends (before the events in the movie) debuted on CBS with many of the original voice actors reprising their roles from the feature, including actress Jodi Benson as Ariel.

However, the first attempt to tell the prequel tales of Ariel was in the hands of talented Jim Henson. From the *Los Angeles Times* on February 25,1990 in an article written by Stacy Smith:

> Kids who couldn't get enough of Disney's *The Little Mermaid* will have plenty of new mermaid adventure stories and music to look forward to if the Disney Channel's daily half-hour *The Little Mermaid's Island* show debuts before year's end, which looks likely.
>
> It's been in the planning stages, says producer John Purdy, since before the animated feature came out. Purdy says that four musical numbers per episode are planned, with ten songwriters already at work.
>
> For the TV version, Ariel the Mermaid will be a real-live lady— actress Marietta Deprima—whose island home and undersea grotto will be inhabited by Jim Henson puppet versions of characters from the film. Sam Wright [Sebastian the Crab] and Buddy Hackett [Scuttle the Seagull] are among those already set to reprise their vocal roles.

Marietta DePrima graduated from Northwestern University in 1986 with a degree in Theater Arts and immediately got a role in an episode of the TV series *Family Ties*. She is probably best known to audiences for her role as "Sally Rogers" in the ABC/UPN sitcom *The Hughleys*. The then twenty-five year old actress married actor George Newbern in 1990, the same year she was working on the pilot for *The Little Mermaid's Island,* and they eventually had three children.

DePrima had an extensive singing background, making her New York debut in the Broadway revival of *Godspell* (and much later singing on the soundtrack for DreamWorks's first animated feature, *Prince of*

Egypt) so she was more than capable of handling the demands for *The Little Mermaid's Island's* new songs.

The only other live performer in the series would be a British colonial ship captain named Grimsby (only called by name in the second episode). Instead of the stuffy, thin adviser and valet to Prince Eric in the original film, this Grimsby was played with a twinkle in his eyes by actor Clive Revill as an obviously well-traveled, well-fed, good-natured seafarer who is accompanied by his huge four-legged Muppet sheepdog, Max.

Max looks like his counterpart in the original film and serves not only as a companion, but a first mate, always tying off the ship to the pier on Mermaid's Island with his mouth. The puppet used for Ambrosius in Jim Henson's film *Labyrinth* (1986) was recycled as Max.

Revill is a well-respected actor of stage, film and television, as well as quite accomplished at doing voice over work for animated cartoons. He seems to be having great fun playing the self-assured captain of a small ship. He is attired in a customized version of a traditional Royal Navy uniform, but with a gold vest and a tri-cornered hat probably to suggest roughly the same time period as the original animated feature.

All the other characters were performed by Muppets modeled after the characters in the original film: Flounder, Scuttle, Sebastian and Ursula's two evil hench-eels, Flotsam and Jetsam. Flotsam and Jetsam are the villains of the show who instead of using physical violence, play seductive mind games to corrupt the good characters into doing something bad (that in the spirit of all Disney Channel shows they learn to overcome and correct by the end of the half hour).

Two new major characters were also featured. Flounder, the little yellow and blue talkative young fish, who was Ariel's best friend apparently had a twin sister named Sandy, who was yellow and pink and had eyelashes. She is only called Sandy in the second episode and appears to be related to Flounder rather than just a random girl fish of the same age.

There was also a full-sized costumed character named Scales. Scales is a musical green dragon with pink highlights on his belly and tail who lives in a rock cave in the center of the island. Near the entrance to the cave is a double keyboard rock piano as well as a table with various pots and pans that Scales (Michael Thompson) uses to create songs.

There are also a lot of miscellaneous Muppet aquatic characters like lobsters, octopus, shark, sea horses and assorted fish. Occasionally, there are some shots of real fish swimming underwater to act as a transition from one scene to another.

The island looks like an old-fashioned keyhole shape at first but closer examination shows that it is two separate bodies of land joined together with a curved rock bridge. That bridge allows the ocean to flow into a large central lagoon and then back out to the sea on the other side.

The smallest section of the island that is closest to the audience has a wooden pier that juts out into the ocean, allowing Grimsby to dock his ship for visits. The pathway to the curved bridge is actually a gigantic keyboard like the one in the Tom Hanks' movie *Big* that lights up and plays music depending where someone steps.

The larger curved side of the island is covered with trees and rocks. In the exact center is a huge rock cave that looks more man-made than a natural phenomenon and this is where Scales lives.

The series would have been done as a partnership between Henson and Disney. The Disney Channel program was aimed at a preschool demographic audience like similar programs including *Welcome to Pooh Corner* and *Dumbo's Circus*.

Basically, DePrima portraying Ariel would interact with the puppet characters and it would all be staged using chroma-key technology so that elaborate backgrounds for the island and under the sea could be incorporated with the real sets in post production.

Ariel's costume was much more modest than the one in the film with its iridescent green scales covering the actress from the top of her chest all the way down to the finny tail.

I talked with Oscar winning Robert Short who told me:

> I designed and created the Mermaid tail costume for *The Little Mermaid's Island*.
>
> Having designed, constructed and supervised Daryl Hannah's mermaid tail and effects for *Splash*, Disney turned to me for this pilot and series. I made the tail from the same material as I had for Daryl's costume, but it was much more modest than the look of Ariel in the animated film.
>
> About the underwater shots of Ariel swimming, we shot the sequence with the actress in the actual tail at the Disney water park, Typhoon Lagoon, in Orlando.
>
> The challenge was not only to create something beautiful but also practical which the actress could swim in below sea level and still look at ease. This was accomplished using a new never-before-used material called Skin-Flex, which became an industry standard.

Filming of the show reportedly took place in a very old studio in the Silverlake district of Los Angeles.

Since this series never aired due to the complications after Henson's untimely death, the two episodes that were completed lack the final opening titles and there is no end credit listing. The post-production on these shows was done over the summer after Henson's passing and delivered to Disney in the fall of 1990 to meet the contractual obligation.

Disney passed on the series for a number of reasons, including probably no longer having access to the Henson team who were removed from all Disney-related projects as soon as they completed any existing commitments.

The half-hour pilot episode was titled *Sebastian's Birthday,* where it is Sebastian's birthday and he is looking for his friends, unaware that they are secretly preparing a surprise birthday party for him.

Sebastian runs into Scuttle the seagull who mistakenly thinks that Sebastian has said that it is "Bird Day." Scuttle's determined confusion and constantly mangling of words was obviously meant to supply humor. In addition, Scuttle was the primary object of physical comedy like bumping his head on the bridge because Sebastian cried out "Duck!" rather than "Seagull!"

As Scuttle leaves, Sebastian breaks into song about his birthday: "It's my B-Day. It's my best day. It's my birthday. It's the day that I was born. It's the day that I began. It's the day that I became...the wonderful crab I am."

He is accompanied by a chorus of pink singing oysters and an unseen steel drum band.

Ariel is in her underwater cave of treasures with Flounder and Sandy, and she has pulled out a one-of-a-kind teacup for Sebastian's birthday gift. When Sebastian arrives and wants them to join him for some fun, they turn him away by singing: "I'm just so busy. So very busy. What a pity I can't come out to play. You'll really have to go now. I'm sorry for you know how much I'd love to have you stay. But I'm busy. Too busy to play."

Sebastain suspects that something is fishy but leaves to visit his friend Scales. On the way he runs into the two eels who try to convince Sebastian that his friends have forgotten his birthday and don't care about him.

Scales is having difficulty because the balloons he has blown up for the party keep popping. To try to distract Sebastian, Scales sings: "Bing! Bang! Bong! Let's play a noisy song."

All this noise give Sebastian a headache and he leaves to sulk in his underwater home after another confrontation with the eels who assure him there is no reason to have friends.

Grimsby and Max dock the ship at the pier and encounter the still confused Scuttle. The captain has brought a three-layer birthday cake for Sebastian's surprise party.

While Max stays to watch the ship, Grimsby and Scuttle dance down the lighted keyboard pathway singing "Surprise! Surprise! I love the unexpected. Two happy guys who never feel dejected...because a big surprise is something we both can share!"

Ariel has accidentally broken the tea cup while trying to wrap it in seaweed and sings:

> Oh dear. It's broken in two. I can't give him this. What will I do..to thank him for all the things he does? To show him I care because he's a friend. Friends new and old are worth more than treasure to me.

With the help of Flounder and Sandy, she thinks of something else to give.

She shows up at the surprise party outside Scales' home along with Scuttle, Scales and Grimsby who has brought not only a cake but candles. He tries ineffectually to explain the concept of birthday candles to Scuttle who originally thought the candles were candy.

Ariel, Flounder and Sandy go to get Sebastian who claims he can't come because he is too busy. They drag him to the party anyway where they all sing a short reprise of the song *B-Day*. Ariel has written Sebastian a poem for his present and Flounder and Sandy have put it into a frame "so he can look at it every day."

The show ends with the sight gag of an ecstatic Sebastian blowing out his candles with such force that the top tier of the cake blows off, covering Scuttle with frosting.

A second episode was completed titled *Tell The Truth*. In her cave of treasures, Ariel is showing Flounder and Sandy her extensive pearl collection that she keeps in a big clam shell.

Showing off, Flounder swims around and knocks over some of Ariel's treasures and then sings:

> Oops. Uh Oh. Never should have played around your stuff I guess.
> Oops. Uh Oh. Everything's scattered and what a mess.

Ariel forgives Flounder but tells him to leave her stuff alone as she goes topside to meet Grimsby who has promised to bring her a special surprise gift. Once she is gone, the eels drop by and try to stir up trouble by suggesting the mermaid is bad because she won't share her things. They goad Flounder into showing them Ariel's pearls which he accidentally knocks over and spills on the floor.

As they clean up the mess, the eels try to convince Flounder and Sandy in song to tell a little fib about what happened:

> When you're stuck in a mess, it's so easy to slip in a little white lie. There's no use in making waves. Why don't you relax? Our advice is be cool as ice, falsify the facts. Who's to know? Who's to care? The truth's not mandatory. It's OK to twist around the story.

Unseen, each of the eels take a pearl and swim off as Flounder and Sandy gather the rest to put back in the shell.

Grimsby has brought a small wrapped package for Ariel from the Spice Islands. After Grimsby docks, Ariel pops up and wants her gift.

Grimsby hears an odd racket coming from the direction of Scales' home and wants to investigate. He tells Ariel and Scuttle to wait and when he returns, they will open the mystery package together.

An impatient Ariel and Scuttle try to guess what is in the wrapped gift and sing their ideas:

> What can it be? What can it be? I just can't wait to see! Curiosity has got the best of me.

Flounder and Sandy have decided to make up a story that a huge orange sea monster's gigantic tail knocked over the pearls they have just finished collecting and put back in the shell. However, they are surprised by Sebastian and knock the pearls on the floor again.

Sebastian sings:

> The moral to the story is very plain to see. There's no need for lies or alibis. All you need is honesty. The truth. The truth. Feels so good to stop lying. The truth is always simple.

Grimsby has discovered Scales bashing different items that have washed up on shore to try to create music because three musical spikes on his tail are broken. Scales sings: "I've got the broken down, tried to play it, makes me angry, I can't fix it blues." Grimsby does fix the bent spikes with "a little bit of patience and little dab of glue."

The eels argue over the two pearls they stole. They fight over who has the largest pearl. Ariel swims by and recovers her two pearls from the ocean floor and swims back to the cave of treasures.

She discovers the truth that Flounder knocked over her pearls while showing off. Flounder swears to never play with Ariel's stuff any more and she accepts the apology.

She has returned to take Flounder, Sandy and Sebastian with her to see Grimsby's surprise gift opened. Unfortunately Scuttle has already opened it. He has also sneezed himself into a barrel on the deck of the ship. The gift was a box of pepper from the Spice Islands to season food.

Ariel and the gang arrive and Scuttle tries to lie that Max made him open the box. Scuttle is convinced to tell the truth and they all sing a short reprise of "The truth. Tell the truth. Feels so good to stop the lying."

Scuttle continues to sneeze uncontrollably in the barrel as this episode ends.

According to Karen Falk, head archivist for the Jim Henson Company:

> The Henson Workshop created the puppets and Ed Christie went out to the shoot to wrangle them, but that was the extent of our involvement. Jim did not direct, produce or perform and was pretty disappointed by the pilot.

The Gray Seal (1958–1962)

Ron Miller, who worked at the Disney Studio as a producer when Walt Disney was alive, told me:

> Walt loved the stories of Jimmie Dale. He would get so enthusiastic that in the halls he would act out the stories of the character who was a gentleman thief. We pitched the idea of a television series with the character to both ABC and later NBC but they turned it down because it was not what the public expected out of a Disney product.
>
> I think one of them asked for a pilot which was standard practice in the industry at the time and Walt replied, "We don't make free samples." But he really wanted to do an adventure series using the character.

Originally signed April 2, 1952, and filed for record on May 19, 1952, Marguerite Pearl Packard, acting on behalf of the late author Frank Packard, freely gave "for valuable consideration paid to the undersigned by Walt Disney Productions" the "sole and exclusive" rights to make "motion picture, photoplay, television, radio and/or any other adaptations of every kind and character" as well as the right to "obtain copyright in all countries upon said work and upon any and all adaptations".

This document was for the rights to "All stories which were written by Frank L. Packard, deceased, utilizing the fictional character, JIMMIE DALE."

Jimmie Dale, the infamous "Gray Seal," was created by Packard (February 2, 1877—February 17, 1942), who was a Canadian novelist born in Montreal, Quebec. He worked as a civil engineer on the Canadian Pacific Railway and his first stories were railroad stories but he earned a living by writing other "pulpish" stories including several Westerns. If he is remembered at all today, it is for his work on his character Jimmie Dale.

Those adventures first appeared in serial installments in *People's Magazine* (and later magazines like *Short Stories Magazine* and *Detective Fiction Weekly Magazine)* before they were later compiled and published in novels: *The Adventures of Jimmie Dale* (1917), *The Further Adventures of Jimmie Dale* (1919), *Jimmie Dale and the Phantom Clue"*(1922), *Jimmie*

Dale and the Blue Envelope Murder (1930) (which is visibly in evidence in a stack of books on Walt's desk in a 1932 publicity photo of him), and *Jimmie Dale and the Missing Hour* (1935).

When the stories first appeared, the *Saturday Review* called them: "Stories of excitement, intrigue, etc., which have no equal."

The New York World said: "These tales are abounding in 'pep'! Beyond doubt the most polished narratives of the underworld yet published."

In fact, the character was so popular that Broadway actor E.K. Lincoln (not to be confused with actor Elmo Lincoln) starred in a 16-chapter silent movie serial titled *Jimmie Dale Alias the Gray Seal* from the Monmouth Film Company distributed through the Mutual exchanges.

Directed by Harry McRae Webster and written by Mildred Considine (based on Packard's stories), the film was released March 23, 1917 and fairly closely followed Packard's concepts including using the mystery woman from the books.

But who was Jimmie Dale?

Walter Gibson, who created the Shadow, claims that he "borrowed" elements for that famous character from Jimmie Dale. Walt had read the serialized adventures when he was a teenager and fell in love with the Gray Seal character. His boyhood friend Walt Pfieffer who later became a storyman at the studio recalled that Walt, a natural actor, would love re-enacting those stories for him.

As Disney executive Donn Tatum told author Bob Thomas in an interview on May 24, 1973:

> He [Walt] also used to talk about… He loved the Gray Seal stories. Do you ever remember that? Jimmie Dale Alias the Gray Seal? He used to pitch that as a television show. The Gray Seal was really sort of an amateur private eye who lived in Boston. His name was Jimmie Dale and Walt used to act them out all the time.
>
> Jimmy Dale was a disguise artist. In every story he'd put on a different disguise and find the criminal. And if he didn't find the criminal he prevented someone from committing a crime. And his trademark was a gray seal pasted somewhere. Walt had bought all the books. There were a number of them and he owned all the rights to them.

According to the Disney Archives, there was a story number (1764) assigned to the "Jimmie Dale project" on December 26, 1951, and John Lucas headed the story crew. This was several months before Walt actually got the rights to the character. However, no other information that can be easily found about the project exists at the Disney Archives other than the project was eventually abandoned some time within the following decade.

Jimmie Dale was the son of a wealthy New York City family. He spent his teenage years working at his father's safe manufacturing factory and later entered Harvard University where he spent a lot of time reading detective fiction and amusing himself with amateur theatrics.

After graduation, he joined the exclusive St. James Club and lived the life of leisure that only a gentleman could. To amuse himself, he created the identity of the "Gray Seal", a two-fisted masked mystery man, who broke into homes, stores and public buildings and opened even the most tightly guarded safes just to prove that no safe was safe. He always left his calling card, a gray diamond paper seal, but never stole anything.

He lived alone in his mansion except for his faithful older butler, Jason, and his devoted but rough chauffeur, Benson. In addition to being the "Gray Seal," he also adopted another secret identity, "Larry the Bat", a disreputable dope fiend who could more easily maneuver through the underworld of crime to obtain information. Later in the series, he creates yet another persona, "Smarlinghue," a junkie-artist.

He kept all his equipment including his disguise kit at a secret hideout on the third floor of a tenement in the worst part of New York, the Bowery. This fortress of solitude is called the "Sanctuary" and it also serves as a refuge for the foppish playboy.

As the Gray Seal, his attire includes a "wide leather belt filled with small pockets," each with the tools of his trade.

Unfortunately, Jimmie made a mistake on one of his playful capers and ended up being blackmailed by a mystery woman known only as "the Tocsin." She later turns out to be Marie LaSalle, a young and beautiful woman, who uses Jimmie's skills to put an end to the crime bosses controlling New York City's criminal organization known as the Crime Club.

After many years of flirtations, Dale and LaSalle walk off into the sunset together once the Crime Club is destroyed.

During these adventures, the Gray Seal developed an adversarial relationship with Herman Carruthers, a former Harvard classmate of Jimmie Dale and editor of the *Morning News-Argus* newspaper.

Packard describes Jimmie's physical appearance in this paragraph: "Six feet he stood, muscular in every line of his body, like a well-trained athlete with no single ounce of superfluous fat about him--the grace and ease of power in his poise. His strong, clean-shaven face, as the light fell upon it now, was serious--a mood that became him well--the firm lips closed, the dark, reliant eyes a little narrowed, a frown on the broad forehead, the square jaw clamped."

Jimmie had an unusual aptitude for all things mechanical and his memory is phenomenal. He is also an accomplished painter, disguise artist and mimic among other talents.

A thief who uses his talents for good? Well, that was the Saint. A gentleman safe cracker? Well, that is probably Raffles. A special utility belt with the tools of the trade? Well, that was Batman. Multiple secret identities? Well, that's the Shadow. A secret lair? Well, that was Doc Savage. Leaving behind a signature icon? Well, that could be the Spider or even the Scarlet Pimpernel (who never left behind flowers in the book but did in his first film outing made long after Jimmie Dale's success) or maybe even Zorro who left the famous "Z."

However, the Gray Seal stories appeared in 1914 when Walt Disney was about thirteen years old and almost two decades before the era of pulp hero and all these other characters that were mentioned in the previous paragraph. The only pulp-like hero to precede the Gray Seal was probably Baroness Orczy's *The Scarlet Pimpernel* (1903).

Jimmie was, in many ways, a model for later classic heroic characters who are now so beloved who made use of secret identities (especially the ineffectual wealthy playboy who becomes a masked two-fisted man of action), secret hideouts, special gadgets, beautiful mystery women who helped them in their endeavors, costumes and disguises, battling with the local newspaper editor, and so many other iconic elements.

Like many teenagers, Walt found a hero he wanted to emulate and that dream stayed with him until his death. It is nice to know that he could occasionally escape into a fantasy world where he was a noble and clever gentleman thief thwarting the criminals of New York.

Abandoned Tomorrowland Shows (1956–1965)

On March 9, 1955, in his introduction to the *Disneyland* weekly television show episode *Man in Space*, Walt Disney said:

> In our modern world, everywhere we look we see the influence science has upon our daily lives. Discoveries that were miracles a few short years ago are accepted as commonplace today. Many of the things that seem impossible now will become realities tomorrow.
>
> One of man's oldest dreams has been the desire for space travel—to travel to other worlds. Until recently, this seemed to be an impossibility, but great new discoveries have brought us to the threshold of a new frontier—the frontier of interplanetary space.

Back in the 1950s, scientist Wernher von Braun believed he could transform the public's fascination with science fiction into an interest in science fact that might spark faster development of a viable American space program. UFO sightings and a flood of science-fiction films preying on post-war paranoia filled the imagination of the American public.

Collier's magazine (which had a weekly circulation of three to four million readers) offered von Braun and scientists like Heinz Haber and Willy Ley an opportunity to write a series of "science factual" articles.

Disney animator Ward Kimball eagerly read these articles. He was in charge of developing the space shows for the Tomorrowland segment of the Disneyland weekly television series. Kimball contacted von Braun to act as a consultant and the scientist leapt at the chance. Von Braun realized that there were fifteen million Americans with television sets and this was a perfect opportunity to "sell" the average American on the exploration of space.

Mike Wright, staff historian for the Marshall Space Flight Center, said:

> To make people believe that space flight was a possibility was his greatest accomplishment. Von Braun brought all of this out of the realm of science fiction.

An estimated forty-two million viewers saw the first Disney Tomorrowland space show, *Man in Space*, when it premiered on March 1955. It was followed by *Man in the Moon* in December 1955 and *Mars and Beyond* in December 1957. These three films are often credited with popularizing the United States government space program in the 1950s.

The films also influenced many people who later became aerospace engineers and even top NASA officials and had a significant cultural impact on the American space program. News articles half seriously suggested that the United States should turn over the space program to Disney since Disney had a plan and a vision.

In March 1961, when Walt talked with reporters about his new *Wonderful World of Color* show on NBC TV, he said that he wasn't going to make any more of the Tomorrowland space shows because they were just too expensive.

Disney executive Donn Tatum, in an interview with writer Richard Hubler, stated:

> Our experience was that they don't have as broad an appeal audience-wise and they are expensive to do and generally speaking the networks and the advertisers, while they didn't have any direct control over what we did, they would prefer things that got a bigger rating.

However, during Walt's lifetime, there were three other Disney space shows intended for the television series that got to various stages of development: "The Project Vanguard Project," "The UFO Show," and "The NASA Show."

The Project Vanguard Project: Moon Watch

Plans for *Mars and Beyond* began as early as 1954, with Kimball hoping the show would be finished by spring 1956. That airdate would coincide with Mars being closest to the Earth. However, the show didn't end up being aired until December 1957. The reason was that Kimball and his team were temporarily sidetracked by another space show that was never made.

The National Academy of Sciences and the Naval Research Laboratory supported a new space program known as Project Vanguard. Von Braun worked on a competing program for the U.S. Army known as Redstone with the Explorer satellite.

For a variety of reasons, the United States government chose to back Project Vanguard, especially since it gave the impression of being more scientific than military. Redstone was more of a public relations risk because of the involvement of Von Braun and his past connections with the German rocketry program during World War II.

The National Academy of Sciences and IBM (who were supplying the computer power for the project) asked Disney to make a film on Project

Vanguard. They wanted the same support and enthusiasm of the American public for their plans as had been generated by the first two space shows. Kimball and his unit were pulled away from finishing up *Mars and Beyond* to concentrate on the timely topic, since the prediction was that the first Vanguard launch would be in the latter part of 1957.

That prediction turned out to be more than a little optimistic. Kimball's team prepared a story again using the information from the experts on the project starting in February 1957. It was tentatively titled "The Artificial Satellite" and later "Moon Watch." Disney was ready to go into production when something happened that immediately cancelled the proposed Disney space episode.

Kimball said:

> I was working on the IBM picture called "Moon Watch" which was going to trace our first Vanguard shuttle, our little satellite, the size of a grapefruit... It was about all the amateur astronomers all over the world would be lining up with their telescopes in a straight line, and if they saw something come overhead that was blinking, pulsating, they would mark the time, and the latitude and the longitude, and so forth, and all that, and then IBM would put it in the computers that filled two or three huge rooms back east plotting the course. This was the Navy Vanguard, and we went back there to Washington and saw the thing. And the Russians fired theirs off and upstaged us.

On October 4, 1957, Russia orbited Sputnik I, the first artificial satellite, and marked the beginning of the "Space Race." Kimball came into the studio and hung a huge black wreath on the storyboards that had been prepared because the Vanguard project was officially dead since it would take at least a year to produce.

A month later, the Russians launched Sputnik II with a dog as a passenger. By the time of Sputnik III, the United States government had reinstated Von Braun's Redstone program, since it seemed that Vanguard would not be ready in the immediate future. Von Braun boldly announced on November 8, 1957, that the United States would have a satellite in orbit within 90 days.

Kimball's crew had gone back to finishing *Mars and Beyond*. Fortunately, all the story meetings and filming sessions with Von Braun had taken place before October. Von Braun no longer had any time for the Disney television show as he raced on presidential orders to put America in space as quickly as possible.

"Mars and Beyond" aired on December 4, 1957.

Two days later, the Vanguard rocket blew up on its launch pad. True to his word, Von Braun successfully launched Explorer I on January

31, 1958. It discovered the Van Allen Radiation Belt. Vanguard I was later successfully launched on March 17, 1958. Of the eleven Vanguard rockets that the project attempted to launch, only three successfully placed satellites into orbit.

Reportedly, the story and notes for the Vanguard Project still reside in the Disney Archives and the abandoned project was all but forgotten—except by the handful of Disney artists who had originally worked on it including Kimball who told me the information.

The UFO Show

At the very end of *Mars and Beyond*, a trio of flying saucers briefly zoom across the screen. Both technical consultants Willy Ley and Heinz Haber had been adamant when they first started working on the Disney space shows that there should be no mention of UFOs. They felt it would undercut the validity of the other material being presented and they were not pleased.

Ward Kimball, who produced and directed all three space shows for the weekly television series, said:

> When Walt came to me asking what we should with the Tomorrowland programs, he said, "You're interested in UFOs and all that stuff..." And I was. I had stacks of books and magazines about UFO sightings and I knew someday I would do something on the subject.

One of Kimball's 1950s cartoons for his *Asinine Alley* panel detailing the trials and tribulations of early motorists in *The Horseless Carriage Gazette* depicts a flying saucer with an intricate hook stealing an old time automobile while the helpless driver is held at ray gun point by a helmeted alien from outer space.

Disney animation director Jack Kinney was originally assigned to do the space programs.

Kimball told Disney historian Michael Barrier, "Jack was not necessarily interested in the fact that we were going out into space, and I was always a UFO fan anyway."

Kimball was given the job and a "blank check" from Walt Disney to do it.

Kimball had placed the flying saucers in the "beyond" section of the television show for several reasons. This episode of the space shows was more speculative than the previous "science-factual" episodes. He also realized that audiences wanted at least a glimpse of a flying saucer, especially with the UFO mania of the time.

However, Kimball hedged his bets because, earlier in the show, this spacecraft had been introduced as a possible future "electromagnetic drive spaceship." Since, in the last scene, Mars had been colonized, it could be assumed that these vehicles were of human origin.

Kimball said:

> Even while I was doing the first three television shows, this [UFOs] was my idea for the fourth Tomorrowland program... that's why you see the animated UFOs taking off at the end of *Mars and Beyond*. I had talked to Walt about this fourth show and what I was thinking about, and he said, "Great, but we've got to get convincing footage!"
>
> We researched some of the incidents where people had taken actual films of flying saucers, and the trail led us to the Air Force establishment.
>
> We were told they had thousands of feet of so-called "alien objects" footage, but that the material was classified. We ran into a brick wall, dressed in khaki uniforms. I went to Walt with the fact that we couldn't get 'smoking gun' footage of UFOs and we both agreed, that was the end of it.

Kimball regaled an audience at the July 1979 MUFON Symposium in San Francisco with his speech about Disney and UFOs. The Mutual UFO Network (MUFON) founded in 1969 is an American nonprofit organization that investigates cases of reported UFO sightings.

Kimball claimed that sometime in the mid-1950s, Walt Disney was contacted by the United States Air Force to cooperate on a documentary about UFOs. In addition, the USAF offered to supply actual UFO footage. However, once work began on the project, the USAF supposedly withdrew the offer to supply film footage.

Kimball claimed that he had personally talked with an Air Force colonel who was the USAF liaison on the project who told him that there was plenty of UFO footage. However, the colonel also emphasized that Disney was not going to be given access to it.

In an interview with Disney Archivist Dave Smith, Kimball said:

> I remember when Al Meyers and [Edward] Heinemann, two big shots in Douglas Aircraft, plus George Hoover, who was head of the office of Naval Research, all came to me and wanted Disney to do a UFO picture. Far-out thinkers, all of them, coming to me and wanting to do a UFO program.
>
> They all knew that UFOs were for real. They had proof; they had everything. And I said, "Sure." I'd been collecting material on UFOs for years anyway, and I had a cupboard full of stuff there. Every report and all the books, you name it. I was a student of Charles Fort (an early investigator of unexplained phenomena), and that was my dream to end the series with Number Four.

> I talked to Colonel Miranda from Wright-Patterson [Air Force Base]. He says, "We've got all sorts of film that we can't show you, it's secret, and it's going to remain classified until we can take one apart and analyze it. Look! Everyone would ask the Air Force, 'What are these things?' And if we couldn't answer that question, we would be in trouble. We could have a war start. They would accuse the Russians of doing it; they're ahead of us." He went through a whole line of reasons why this couldn't be divulged.
>
> He said, "We have shots taken from gun cameras; we have beautiful footage. We've got 'em all shapes and size, port holes, lights. … We don't know what they are yet. Until we can dissect it, and give a reasonable explanation without our society coming unglued, we can't. It's going to remain classified."
>
> It would have been a wonderful show. And I had everything up to the last ten minutes. I had the rendering, and we had these drawings that people have made, the spaceships that had passed for a good part of a day over the Egyptian army in Egypt in 2000 B.C. They described the stench and the fumes, the whole thing; it was even done in hieroglyphics. We wanted to bring that to life. Great thing, you know. Pictorially, it was a wonderful thing to do. But we didn't have that last ten minutes.

Walt was also probably well aware of the fact that while the first show had cost $250,000 to produce but by the time of the final show about Mars, the costs had risen to $450,000 because of the need of original animation to fill in the gaps for missing live action. The UFO show would have been even more expensive to generate new footage.

The NASA Show: Man in Space Then and Now

In 1964, roughly ten years after *Man in Space* aired, Werhner von Braun once again found himself frustrated by the U.S. government's current lack of enthusiasm about putting a man on the moon and, once again, von Braun saw that the solution was to involve Walt Disney.

Von Braun wrote to Bill Bosche, a sketch artist and writer on the earlier Disney space films with whom von Braun had worked closely. It was Bosche who sent von Braun long lists of technical questions that needed to be answered in order to develop the storyboards for the show.

Bosche was an artist, writer, and producer at Disney for more than thirty years. In the letter, von Braun invited Walt and other key Disney personnel to tour the Marshall Space Flight Center in Huntsville, Alabama.

Von Braun, who was then director of NASA's space flight center in Huntsville, wrote:

It is really only a few short years ago since I had the pleasure of working at your studios [on a project] which, it turns out was quite prophetic.

I understand that over the years you have kept up a rather lively interest in the space program and, particularly, in manned space flight. For this reason, I thought you might like to have an opportunity to see just how prophetic [you were].

It was apparent that von Braun was hoping lightning would strike twice and that he could get Walt so excited about what they were doing that it might generate another series of Disney television programs to enthuse the public to actively support a more aggressive space program.

Frank Williams, director of the Future Projects Office and a close associate of von Braun, wrote to Bart Slattery, director of the Public Affairs Office at the Marshall Space Flight Center, on November 13, 1964 that:

Out of this we would at least establish good will, and maybe (if we play our cards right) we could get something going that would be of tremendous benefit to MSFC, Apollo, NASA, and the entire space effort.

In April 1965, Walt Disney, accompanied by his brother Roy, as well as several WED Enterprise personnel—including Bill Bosche, Ken Peterson, John Hench, Claude Coats and Ken O'Connor—visited the three chief space centers at Houston, Cape Kennedy and Huntsville.

Walt took time out between his looking around to fly a couple of simulators. His earth-bound flight missions were both accomplished at NASA's manned spacecraft center at Houston. There, Walt at the age of 63 "flew" a Gemini simulator to a successful space rendezvous or docking, then "landed" on the moon in a LEM (lunar excursion module) after two professional airplane pilots had well overshot the green-dot target area on a simulated moon.

Without any previous experience, Walt had to quickly learn to operate and "fire" the retro-rockets which provide capsule control, accounting for drift and the other momentum factors that plague spacemen.

On the front page of the April 13, 1965 edition of *The Huntsville Times* with a headline proclaiming "Walt Disney Makes Pledge to Aid Space," Walt was quoted as saying:

If I can help through my TV shows ... to wake people up to the fact we've got to keep exploring, I'll do it.

Von Braun's daily journal entry for April 13, 1965, indicated his hope that the tour "may easily result in a Disney picture about manned space flight."

However, if von Braun was hoping that Walt would immediately put such a project into the works, he was sadly disappointed. Walt's attention was consumed with other projects. While Walt may have had an interest in space exploration, he was passionate about Epcot Center, Cal Arts, Mineral King and a half dozen other projects that took precedence over developing another space series.

Disney executive Card Walker told interviewer Richard Hubler:

> [Walt] made a trip down to Houston, down to Cape Canaveral and all that through Wernher Von Braun to see the space program, the astronaut training and all that, and then went down to the space program at Kennedy and what they were doing.
>
> He was mulling this thing, we hadn't got it started, but he was ready to make a film to show the peace benefits that would come with the development of atomic energy. The government was interested, Wernher was interested—[Walt] just didn't get around to it. But that would have been the next step.

Von Braun became seriously in 1975 and on June 16, 1977, succumbed to cancer at sixty-five years of age.

Former Disney archivist Dave Smith discovered in the inactive story file a project titled *Man in Space: Then and Now*. Smith interviewed Bill Bosche about what happened to the project that was never made.

Bosche recalled:

> One of the reasons was that Von Braun became ill. And he visited us here. This was a project that I had started and Von Braun did visit us here at one time and we talked about it and the idea was to use footage and use Von Braun from the old show and some things that he had predicted then and how it had turned out and then let him make predictions for the future.
>
> And because of other production commitments and things like that it just never really got off the ground. And it would have been a fairly expensive show. I still think it would have been fun to do.

Hansel and Gretel (1966)

The story of Hansel and Gretel is a well known cautionary German folk tale first recorded and published by the Brothers Grimm in 1812. It tells the tale of a young brother and sister lost in the woods who are tricked by a cannibalistic witch into her house made of tasty sugary confections, like gingerbread, cakes and candy. The witch intends to cook and eat the children but Gretel shoves her into her own oven and the children escape.

Composer Engelbert Humperdinck wrote an opera about the story in 1893 because his sister wanted to put on a children's play based on the tale. He became so involved with the project that it expanded into a full opera for both children and adults.

Walt Disney had tackled the story earlier in the 1932 Silly Symphony *Babes in the Woods*. Walt altered the original fairy tale significantly even including some happy, bearded dwarfs in matching red outfits who help save the children and having the witch, who earlier was able to fly in the sky with a magic broom like traditional witches but not in the original story, slip by herself into her boiling cauldron and not be pushed by Gretel.

It was the third Disney animated short made in Technicolor and the first attempt by Disney to do a "serious" adaptation of a classic fairy tale. The witch was voiced by Lucille La Verne who would later go on to voice the Queen and Old Hag in *Snow White and the Seven Dwarfs* (1937). At some point in the 1930s, the story of Hansel and Gretel was briefly considered as a possible animated feature with artist Albert Hurter creating some concept sketches for the film.

It would be three decades before Walt seriously decided to take another look at the story that he had also once considered adapting into a short with Mickey Mouse as Hansel and Minnie as Gretel. Concept art still survives of that proposal, as well. Later, Mickey and Minnie did star in a version of Hansel and Gretel for the Disney House of Mouse 2002 Halloween special *Mickey's House of Villiains*.

In 1961, Disney executive Jack Cutting sent a series of memos to Walt about the purchase of the rights to the Humperdinck opera but Walt wanted to do something original.

In 1964, Disneyland Records released a 33 1/3 rpm long playing album *Walt Disney Presents The Story of Hansel and Gretel* using the music from the opera by Humperdinck. The cast included Laura Olsher as the narrator, Michael Donahue as Hansel, Ann Jillian as Gretel and Martha Wentworth as the witch. The album also featured the singing voices of Marni Nixon, Sally Sweetland and Kathleen De Spain.

However, Walt still thought the story could be made into a film musical. Composer Richard Sherman recalled in the book *Walt's Time: From Before to Beyond*:

> Walt learned his lessons with *Babes In Toyland* in 1961 and applied those lessons to *Mary Poppins* in 1964. He followed Poppins with *The Happiest Millionaire,* and ultimately we [the Sherman Brothers] completed *The One and Only, Genuine, Original Family Band* and *Bedknobs and Broomsticks*.
>
> But along the way, we also worked on a now legendary 'lost' Disney live-action musical, *Hansel and Gretel*.
>
> It was early 1966 when Walt paired us once again with screenwriter A.J. Carothers with whom we were just finishing *The Happiest Millionaire*. Also joining us from the *Millionaire* team were producer Bill Anderson, director Norman Tokar and the delightful Geraldine Page who had tentatively agreed to play the role of the witch.
>
> *Hansel and Gretel* wasn't headed for the theaters though. It was envisioned as a 90-minute live-action television special. And that, we believe was to be its ultimate undoing.
>
> The project came together quickly. By September, we had completed six songs to accompany AJ's script and the pre-production process had begun. It didn't take long before it became apparent to the sharp pencil people that *Hansel and Gretel* would be an expensive project to produce—besides the inherent higher costs of a musical, the story called for plenty of intricate special effects.
>
> As the critical "go/no go" decision approached, we lost Walt, the one person at the Studio who could see past the bottom line. In the crazy and uncoordinated months that followed Walt's death, *Hansel and Gretel* was cancelled and [almost] forgotten.

Hansel and Gretel was production number 7252 with a working draft completed by September 27, 1967. Besides *Millionaire*, Carothers worked at Disney for roughly seven years, writing scripts for *Miracle of the White Stallions* (1963) and *Emil and the Detectives* (1964), among other Disney work including *Never a Dull Moment* (1968).

Carothers was the creator of *The Nanny and the Professor* television series, wrote the story for Michael J. Fox's film *The Secret of My Success* (1987) and was responsible for the scripts for more than 100 motion pictures, television shows and plays. One of his final works was writing the book for the Sherman Brothers stage musical *Piccadilly* in 1996.

Carothers' draft eliminated the cruel stepmother who, because it was a time of famine in the original tale, had sent her two children off into the forest so that she and her husband wouldn't starve. So, like many Disney stories, the mother was gone and the father struggled to take care of his two young children.

It is especially challenging because the children are rebellious and not well-behaved. The story opens with them wreaking havoc on their newest housekeeper who finally gets so fed up that she quits.

The father is a woodcutter and is away most of the day so needs a housekeeper to watch over the young Hansel and Gretel. Deep in his heart, he knows that what they really need is a mother and what would fill the hole in his own heart is a new wife. However, he realizes that is just a dream and doesn't know what else he can do to handle his two children.

One day while chopping wood in the forest, he thinks he sees a beautiful maiden wandering through the trees. He drops his axe and tries to follow her but she is always temptingly just ahead of him out of reach.

He arrives at a waterfall that he has never seen before that is cascading into a tranquil pool. He can no longer see any sign of the mysterious woman so stoops down to take a drink from the pool to refresh himself.

As he stares into the water, he sees her face appear briefly in a reflection but a bird flies down and disturbs the surface of the water and the image disappears. He gets up and looks around but sees no one.

However, all of this activity is being watched by a witch in her crystal ball. The one power in the entire universe she has been unable to obtain is true love. With that one missing element, she could rule the world...somehow not clearly explained.

She understands that she cannot steal love. True love must be freely given. She decides that perhaps she can trick this love-sick woodcutter into giving her the gift of true love. Unfortunately, her wickedness has made her exterior just as misshapen and ugly as her interior.

Using magic, she transforms herself into a beautiful young woman, similar, but not exact, to the one the woodcutter was chasing. She appears at his cottage and uses her guile to become the new housekeeper, an offer the man eagerly accepts.

Hansel and Gretel are still a handful and they spitefully keep interfering with the witch's attempts to woo their father into giving her true love. The witch decides that she must get rid of these two brats if she is to get what she wants.

She tricks them into going into the forest where they get lost. A group of helpful animals sing to them: "Chin up/ You'll be happy hearted / Once you get it started/ Up with your chinny chin chin!"

The witch's cottage deep in the forest is the traditional gingerbread house from the classic fairy tale decorated with tempting sweets of every kind so the children enter. They find themselves trapped in a house that looks more like a mad scientist's frightening laboratory filled with an army of demons who are described as "grotesque creatures who dance with delight" at seeing their future feast.

The witch transforms back into her true sickly green identity and reunites with her talking raven who unlike the one in *Sleeping Beauty* (1959) is capable of speaking words clearly. It would probably have been done as an elaborate audio-animatronics character.

A battle of wits and a massive physical battle ensues between the children inside the cottage and the witch including lightning bolts, furniture magically flown to the ceiling so the children can't hide and even an extended scene with them shrunk in size and dashing around the cottage and its devices.

The special effects were extensive, including the need for the witch's flying broom since, like in the Silly Symphony, she utilized that mode of transportation. Being a Disney film, Gretel would not have shoved the witch into the oven to burn in horrible agony. The witch herself slips into the oven and is baked into gingerbread cookies.

Obviously, this draft was in need of Walt's story-editing skills.

Tentatively, Matthew Garber and Karen Dotrice, the child stars of *Mary Poppins* (1964) and *The Gnome Mobile* (1967), were seriously considered and then it was decided they would be too old for the roles.

Bill Anderson, Norman Tokar, the Sherman Brothers and AJ Carothers were in New York for the premiere of the film *The Happiest Millionaire* in New York. Actress Geraldine Page (who would later supply the voice of Madame Medusa in the 1977 animated feature *The Rescuers)* was in the film playing the mother of John Davidson's character and, while doing publicity at the premiere, the group got together and Page tentatively agreed to play the witch.

However, even with a script and production team in place and pre-production beginning, some executives at the studio did not share the same enthusiasm for the project as Walt did, especially when it was going to be so expensive.

Since Walt had died in December 1966, the project no longer had a champion and the project simply disappeared from the production schedule.

The Sherman Brothers composed six songs for the musical. The witch would have sung two songs. The woodcutter would have sung "Guardian Star" and the love ballad called "Love Is..." ("Love is the crowning glory/There's no way to count its worth/ But when you wear its golden crown/ You're the richest man on earth!").

The two children also had a song ("If I Could Be What I'd Like to Be").

Richard Sherman once told me, "It should have been made. It would have been wonderful."

Almost equally as "lost" as the proposed feature musical was a thirty-five minute live action Disney television special of the story of Hansel and Gretel directed by Tim Burton and written by Julie Hickson that aired only once on the Disney Channel on Halloween night October 31, 1983 on the series Walt Disney Studio Showcase.

A recently discovered and restored version has only been shown a handful of other times over the decades at Tim Burton retrospective film shows around the world. The Disney Channel magazine indicated another airing was scheduled for October 29, 1983 but there is no confirmation that it was shown. Supposedly Burton was embarrassed by the final production and Disney executives found it too dark and disturbing.

To promote the show on April 26th 1983 the Walt Disney Studio Showcase had an episode entitled *Backstage at Disney* with animation historian John Culhane. The show included a three minute segment of Burton and production designer Rick Henrichs discussing their films *Vincent* and *Hansel and Gretel*.

Costing $116,000 and filmed on 16mm film, the live-action *Hansel and Gretel* special featured a cast of Asian amateur actors, Japanese toys and kung fu fights blended with Burton's distinctive designs working with Heinrichs who made the three-dimensional models.

It reflected Burton's interest in Japanese toys (which is why he made the father a toymaker rather than the traditional woodsman) and the Godzilla movies and featured highly stylized, surrealistic sets familiar to fans of Burton's work. The production incorporated puppets, forced perspective and some stop motion animation.

It had a short, live introduction by actor Vincent Price because the showing also included the Burton stop motion animated short *Vincent* narrated by Price so that the entire program would be forty-five minutes long. The music for the special was done by John Costa who was the music director for the television series *Mr. Rogers' Neighborhood* for approximately thirty years.

The story follows the traditional tale with unexpected Burton twists.

A poor toymaker (Jim Ishida) and his son and daughter (Andy Lee and Allison Hong) suffer under the toymaker's wicked new wife (Michael Yama) who hates Hansel and Gretel. During an altercation during dinner, the two children are sent to their dark attic bedroom where their father later comes and tries to cheer them up with a performance by a small clown puppet named Jocko and a few cookies. He also leaves a small toy swan to watch over them.

The next morning, the stepmother tries to lose the children in the forest but they find their way home thanks to some small stones Hansel has dropped along the way. The next day while the father is in town trying to sell his toys, the stepmother again tries to lose them in the forest. She gives them a toy duck that eats the trail of stones they leave behind them to help find their way home.

While they are sleeping at night in the forest, the toy duck transforms into a small toy robot that leads them to a house made of gingerbread and candy that oozes out of its walls. The witch with a curved candy cane nose (also played by Michael Yama who played the stepmother) who lives there lures them inside with promises of sweet treats. She tells them the furniture like the chairs and table are real candy and the two children greedily enjoy devouring them completely.

Tired, they are led by the witch to two marshmallow beds that capture them with candy cane arms. The bed drops Hansel into a large room with a huge mobile of Dan Dan, the gingerbread man, (a puppet voiced by David Koenigsberg) who insists Hansel eat him so that Hansel will be fattened up for the witch's meal. Hansel does eat some of the gingerbread man but comes to his senses and shatters the creepy clown's head into pieces.

Meanwhile, the witch has taken Gretel down to the kitchen to help heating the oven to bake Hansel. Two long candy cane arms drop from the mobile above Hansel and bring him to the kitchen. Before he can be put into the oven, Gretel grabs the fire iron and hits the witch with it. The witch and Gretel engage in a kung fu style battle using cookie cutters, candy cane nunchucks and throwing star cookies. Hansel breaks free to join the fight.

When the witch makes a flying kick, the children duck out of the way and she flies into her own oven and is trapped. The house begins to melt into a pool of colored frosting while Hansel and Gretel escape just in time.

A toy swan their father had given them earlier appears out of the melted candy and enlarges into the form of a boat and takes the children back home. The father explains that their wicked stepmother is gone for good which is why it is so quiet now. The swan boat begins to spout gold coins from its mouth providing the money the poor family needed to live happily ever after.

Dreamfinders (1983)

The Disney Channel was born in spring of 1983 and, despite the backlog of Disney cartoons and television shows and films the Disney Channel still needed more programming to fill its proposed schedule.

The plan was to balance the programming with one third existing Disney material, one third original programming and one third material that had been acquired from outside sources but was in "keeping with the Disney identity and values".

For Epcot's Future World, Imagineer Tony Baxter created Figment and Dreamfinder who were to be the spokes-figures for the new park. The little winged purple dragon, Figment, was the physical representation of being "a figment of the Imagination."

Dreamfinder was his husky human companion and friend with a full red beard, long blue coat, black top hat and broad smile (supposedly modeled after the physical appearance of Imagineer Joe Rohde at the time).

Figment and Dreamfinder were actually born in a concept for a planned-but-never-built section of Disneyland to be called Discovery Bay in 1976. In that area, there was to be Professor Marvel's Gallery of Illusion, where an audio-animatronics Professor Marvel would display all manner of oddities that he had collected including his collection of dragons.

When that project was cancelled, the professor and one of his little dragons were modified into Dreamfinder and Figment. They would fly in a zeppelin-like flying contraption called the Dreamcatcher to catch ideas and bring them back to their home called the Dream Port.

So that year the Disney Channel debuted, it prepared five episodes of an original one hour show (in three acts) called *Dreamfinders,* with actor Jack Kruschen performing the character of Dreamfinder created for the Journey Into Imagination attraction at Epcot and the character of Eli.

Kruschen was a well-known character actor who received an Oscar nomination for best supporting actor for his 1960 role in Billy Wilder's comedy *The Apartment* and might be remembered by some as having played the Greek grandfathers in the 1980s sitcoms *Webster* and *Full House*.

Peggy Christianson, vice president of Program Development for the channel, said:

We hope this show will help children become more aware of their own creative resources. The main characters are Dreamfinder and Figment, a little dragon, who travel in the dream machine at Epcot Center to explore the creative process.

The show will have elaborate sets and a variety of characters and story lines to convey to children some of the elements involved in creativity, imagination and problem-solving in the largest sense. We really want adults and children to sit down and watch the Disney Channel together.

Walt Disney never aimed at children alone. He always aimed at entertaining a family audience with a quality product and positive values that would appeal to people of all ages.

Supposedly, three episodes were completely scripted but Disney Archivist Dave Smith claimed none were ever filmed although it is clear they were scheduled to be shown by all the promotional advertising.

It has been claimed that at least one episode or part of it was filmed which is where the images for some of the advertising originated. A short appearance (non speaking) of the fully costumed Dreamfinder during the Disney Channel's launch countdown on April 18, 1983 premiering all the upcoming shows was aired.

The show was aimed at youngsters six to twelve and, as previously stated, focused on creativity, problem solving and, of course, imagination.

According to the publicity release:

Imagination unleashed! Colorful characters, seven wildly imaginative sets and a dazzling array of special effects make *Dreamfinders* a one-of-a-kind television experience your entire family will love!

Each episode finds a cast of children in a "real world" setting confronted with a perplexing dilemma. Old Eli, the all-knowing Dreamfinder, whisks the children away on a magical journey to "The Realm of Imagination." There, free of worldly constraints, the children use their ideas and dreams to find a creative solution to their problem.

The journey is not without peril. Travelers through Imagination are always fair prey for the ever present villain Fear and his minions. They persistently attempt to lead Old Eli and the children into the abyss of "Bewilderness."

Created especially for young people by the Disney Imagineers, *Dreamfinders* is a weekly one hour adventure about the imagination and creativity in us all. Friday 2:30pm, Saturday 7:00 am and Sunday 9:00 am."

The premise of the series was that, after school, four children of different ages (one of whom was young actress Kristy Swanson in her first role) dropped by to visit with Dreamfinder. He had an elaborate laboratory that would help to expand imaginations, including a "Door from Here to There" where they could enter and journey anywhere. The famous Dream Catcher blimp would also dock at the Dream Port.

Figment appeared as an elaborate puppet (as he did at Epcot when it opened in 1982 with a walkaround costumed Dreamfinder character manipulating him) but supposedly would also appear in short animated clips where he fought an ugly green creature known as "Fear" and "other villains who lurk in the Bewilderness. The road is challenging but the rewards are many. And our young viewers will see how today's Dreamfinders can become tomorrow's world builders."

The series was produced by Norton Wright, who later went on to be one of the producers on *Sesame Street*. In the series, Dreamfinder was also in evidence in the "real world" as book store owner "Old Eli" perhaps as a reference to Walt "Elias" Disney.

Doug Williams, who wrote the first episode, *Just In Time*, claimed:

> I wrote a script for the show in 1982. No shows were ever aired. Just as the show was building a head of steam Michael Eisner took over as head of Disney Studios and shut down production, for no apparent reason, other than that was/is common practice for when there's a change of power.
>
> That was an unfortunate decision. *Dreamfinders* had great potential to be a fun, educational show with terrific commercial potential. It's possible two or three shows were produced before Eisner shut down production for good.
>
> *Dreamfinders* could have been a good entertaining and informative show for the kids. I doubt that any of the shows that were shot, if they actually were, were ever shown on TV. I suspect that none were ever shown because suppose the audience actually really liked the show? Eisner would have looked like an idiot. Also the story editors claimed they couldn't get good scripts.
>
> The actual production company in charge of making the show was Jess and Company Productions Inc. The producer I worked with was Steve Gertz. I remember walking around the completed set. It was pretty cool. Really a shame it didn't get a chance.

Here are the recurring characters that were to be in each episode:

- Dreamfinder: An amiable man who lives in the Realm of Imagination with his pal, Figment, an animated, dizzy, lovable Dragon.
- Eli: A kindly man, age around 40, who owns a book store; a great friend to all. He's played by the same actor who plays Dreamfinder.

- The Kids: (age 10–12) Tracy (a spoiled girl who really loves money), Nick, Ernest, Jennifer, and Danny. Their clubhouse where they meet is a spare room at Eli's book store.
- Polly: A smart, studious woman who works at the Sci Tech Building in the Realm and often helps Dreamfinder at the Dream Port.
- Curio: An eccentric artist who works in the Artrium in the Realm of the Imagination.
- Fear: A sinister character who raises havoc in the Realm and lives in the Bewilderness.
- Monkey Wrench: A mechanical, goofy monkey who is a member of Fear's mischievous gang.
- Doubting Thomas: A hopelessly confused member of Fear's gang.
- Dream Port: Where the amazing dream vehicle is kept.
- Bewilderness: A dark, foreboding forest in the Realm that is to be avoided; where Fear and his troublesome minions live.

Here is the synopsis for *Just In Time:*

The kids are preparing a surprise birthday party for Eli and are making him presents instead of just buying him something from the mall. Tracy feels it would be easier to just buy something. This leads into a segment about craftspeople who still make things by hand.

Dreamfinder is looking through his telescope at a shower of sparks, ideas that were once in people's brains before they slipped their minds like birth dates, names of people, things that went missing, things they wanted to say but forgot. There are also dark, black thoughts that should be forgotten.

Dreamfinder and Figment intend to go out and capture all the bright, good thoughts but Fear and his minions Monkey Wrench and Doubting Thomas come up with a diabolical plan to stop them. "No good can come from good thoughts," claims Fear.

Polly helps Dreamfinder through mathematical calculations determine the time he needs to leave to capture the thoughts because they are already picking up speed and may disappear forever.

Tracy has lost her wallet with all her money which sparks a segment where Eli talks to her about money: its history, how it is made, the theory behind it and more.

He finishes by saying "Sometimes problems can have more than one solution. Give your problem at little more thought and a different solution might come to mind. Be creative."

The Sci Tech Hall of Time is filled with nothing but all sorts of different clocks. Polly is shining one of the grandest clocks when Doubting Thomas comes in with a beautiful clock to donate to the Hall of Time. It is placed next to the official Realm clock that keeps perfect universal time and all the other clocks are set to it. At the Dream Port, Tracy arrives because she has been trying to dream of a solution to her problem. Dreamfinder explains that he has no money because in the Realm no one buys or sells things. Money is meaningless because they just give people want they need.

Figment suggests that Tracy's answer to where her missing wallet might be is in the shower of fleeting thoughts. She follows Dreamfinder and Figment to the Sci Tech building with all its clocks. This spurs Polly to do a segment about clocks: their history, how they are made, and future clocks.

The gift clock stars smoking and shaking violently and Fear's face appears on the clock face. The clock explodes filling the room with smoke. Polly turns on a fan. Figment gets a fire extinguisher. When the smoke clears, all the clocks have been destroyed and even the computer that Polly uses.

Dreamfinder has hidden another official clock but can't remember where. Dreamfinder and Figment return to the Dream Port to search. Tracy is sent to talk to Curio at the Artrium to find out if he knows the location. Polly starts re-doing calculations by hand.

Ernest, Nick, Jennifer and Danny are already visiting Curio who is dressed like Michelangelo because he is about to paint the Artrium ceiling. The kids have come to the Realm to get some ideas about what presents to make for Eli.

Tracy rushes in to explain that Fear has destroyed all the clocks and ask if Curio knows where the back-up clock is. He doesn't but says he can repair the clocks. Tracy explains the urgency of Dreamfinder having to leave at the exact right time to catch the shower of fleeting thoughts before they are lost forever.

They all rush out to search the Realm for the hidden clock. In the Bewilderness, Fear and his two minions watch all of this on Fear's magic medallion and Fear decides to whisper in the kids' ears.

At the Dream Port, Polly is finishing her calculations and Dreamfinder with a wrench is underneath the Dream Vehicle. "I wish I could remember where I put that clock," says Dreamfinder. "I guess when a guy reaches 55,000 years, he gets a little forgetful." Nick, Danny and Ernest are looking behind trees and in bushes for the hidden clock. Jennifer, Tracy and Curio enter and share that they haven't found anything either. Curio decides to search the basement of the Sci Tech Building thinking it might be hidden in all the junk. He tells the kids to continue searching the forest.

They hear a voice that sounds like Dreamfinder's voice telling them that he found the clock and to come to him in the Bewilderness to help carry the clock.

Tracy suddenly realizes that Dreamfinder is supposed to be in the Dream Port and he would never hide the clock in the Bewilderness. The other kids run into the Bewilderness but Tracy runs back to the Dream Port. Of course, it is Fear imitating Dreamfinder's voice.

At the Dream Port, Tracy finds Dreamfinder and tells him what has happened. Dreamfinder realizes immediately it must be the work of Fear and he needs to go and rescue the kids even if it means missing his launch time.

Tracy and Figment stay and walk by a stream. Seeing the sun in the water, Tracy gets an idea and runs off to the Sci Tech Building to rummage through some junk. In the Bewilderness, Fear keeps moving deeper and deeper away from the kids while still calling out to them.

Dreamfinder and Polly appear before the kids and hug them. In the background, they hear Fear's hideous cackle. "He's just trying to scare you because that's what he does," says Dreamfinder.

When they all return to the Dream Port, including Curio, they find that Tracy is making a sundial that will help them tell the time. She remembered about sundials from Polly's lecture.

Watching on his medallion, Fear is angry about the sundial and decides to scare all the clouds in the sky to block the sun so the sundial won't work. As the clouds gather, Curio tells the kids to imagine the clouds parting and the sun shining through to create the necessary shadow on the sundial. They do and it works.

The Dream Vehicle is able to take off at the exact right moment. Figment is eating a bag of potato chips but he is still able to get the dream vacuum operating just in time. They accomplish their mission and return to the Dream Port. Everyone cheers except for Fear and his minions who hate happy endings.

The tag for the episode is at the Clubhouse. The kids except for Ernest and Tracy are in the darkened room with the table covered with presents. They jump out to surprise the person entering but it turns out to be Tracy. They all hide again.

Outside they hear Ernest thanking Eli for helping him carry a box of books to the Clubhouse. When the lights go on, Eli pretends to be surprised. He unwraps Tracy's gift first. It is the sundial she made in the Realm. Tracy also found her wallet and they all found the back-up clock.

Before ice cream and cake, Ernest inspects Tracy's wallet and laughs when he tells everyone that it says inside of it "handmade in New Mexico."

The Walt Disney Biography Mini-Series (1988)

After the passing of Walt Disney in December 1966, the Disney Company struggled with how to preserve and share the inspirational story of their founder. Author Richard Hubler interviewed dozens of people who knew and worked with Walt and tried putting together a written biography during 1967-1968 but the company did not care for it and gave no reason for its dissatisfaction.

Then writer Lawrence Watkin who had supplied some screenplays for Disney live action films attempted to do a biography but his finished manuscript was also rejected. Finally, newspaper columnist Bob Thomas wrote a biography in 1976 entitled *Walt Disney: An American Original* which is still considered an outstanding and accurate book today by both the Walt Disney Company and the Walt Disney Family Foundation.

Over the decades, the Disney Company has also tried to produce a film or a television series that would tell Walt's story.

The Walt Disney Story in the 500 seat Opera House at Disneyland opened on April 8, 1973 and that same month at Walt Disney World as well.

The finale was a twenty-eight minute biographical film of Walt Disney's personal and professional life from his birth to the creation of the Florida Project that included rare stills and film clips was a project that began in June 1969.

A staff of more than 200 people at Walt Disney Productions pored over 75 hours of interviews conducted with Walt before his untimely death on December 15, 1966.

Bill Bosche, an artist and producer who worked for Disney for more than thirty years supervised the work. By using excerpts from these interviews, in particular the extensive 1956 ones done with *Saturday Evening Post* writer Pete Martin, Walt Disney posthumously narrated much of his own autobiography.

At Disney MGM Studios in Florida as part of the 100 Years of Magic celebration honoring the birth of Walt Disney, an attraction called One Man's Dream opened on October 1, 2001. The finale was a fifteen minute film that tells the story of Walt Disney's life, once again using vintage audio interviews with him. Originally narrated by then CEO Michael Eisner, he was replaced when Eisner left the company in 2005 with actress Julie Andrews.

Senior Show Producer/Director Roger Holzberg of Walt Disney Imagineering said:

> This tells the story of Walt the man, and we hope that guests will be moved by the scope of his imagination, what he accomplished, and what he inspired.

Walt Disney Productions President Ron Miller (husband of Diane Disney Miller, Walt's oldest daughter) told *TV Guide* in the February 21, 1981 issue that the Disney Studio was working on several specials and at least a dozen pilots for the upcoming television season.

Included on the list was *Walt Disney: The Man, The Artist, The Dreamer,* a series of three documentaries on the evolution of the late movie pioneer's dreams and his accomplishments. One episode would be focused on Walt himself, another on his artistic accomplishments and finally his visionary dreams like Disneyland and Epcot. It was to be produced by Dwight Hemion and Gary Smith.

Could that elaborate project have then developed into that star-studded, musical two hour special, *Walt Disney: One Man's Dream* produced by Hemion and Smith that aired December 12, 1981 primarily to promote the opening of Epcot Center? In flashback segments about Walt's life, Christian Hoff played the young Walt Disney and Angus Scrimm played his father, Elias.

It was written by Stan Hart, John McGreevey and Mitzie Welch and directed by Phil May.

When the Disney Channel premiered in 1983, one of its most popular half hour series was the *Disney Family Album* produced by Michael Bonifer and Cardon Walker Jr. by their MICA (<u>Mi</u>chael and <u>Ca</u>rd) Productions. Bonifer did much of the writing and directing of the individual episodes. The success of the series prompted the MICA production company to pitch the idea of a four part television mini-series on the life of Walt Disney.

I interviewed Bonifer in 2010 and he told me:

> I wanted to make Walt Disney's life story and Jim Jimirro [the founding president of the Disney Channel] decided it should be a mini-series. I wrote a four-part mini-series with L.G. Weaver, who was my co-author on that book about Notre Dame football, *Out of Bounds.*
>
> The script was 500 pages long and the Disney Archives has a copy. I put two years into that project. Traveled to places where Walt lived. Talked to people who had known Walt like Clem Flickinger,

Rush Johnson, Hazel George and so many more. I talked with Hazel [the Disney Studio nurse and Walt's confidante] on her deathbed and she told me everything from the first day she met Walt up to his death. There are certain things in the script that don't exist anywhere else.

Then Michael Eisner came on board. His reader, Chris Vogler called me up and said, 'I shouldn't be doing this but wanted to tell you that this is the best thing I ever read.' Vogler later went on to author the book *The Screenwriter's Journey*. So it was not surprising when Cardon [Walker Jr., his producing partne] and I went in to see Eisner and he was all excited about the script and we thought it was going into production.

He gave a few notes and wanted a final polish. However, around that time, Eisner was on the cover of *Time* magazine [April 1988] and he was being hailed as the new Disney and suddenly he started putting roadblocks in the way of the project. As the new Disney, he didn't want comparison with the original.

I know for a fact that he screened episodes of *Disney Family Album* for his new executives but was using it as an example of where he didn't want the brand to be. He wanted to revitalize the brand and not just reminisce about past triumphs. So the project died and that's when I decided to leave.

There were other issues that prevented the mini-series from being made, including lack of support from the Disney family for the project; Roy E. Disney feeling there was not enough about his father in the script and the leadership changing at the Disney Channel who were no longer interested in the project.

Four actors would have been cast in the roles of Walt at various stages of his life. Bonifer envisioned actor Kevin Kline playing Walt for one or more segments of the latter segments. Sam McKim drew the storyboards for the project and those are also in the Disney Archives.

PART FOUR

Animation That Never Was

Over the decades, hundreds of Disney animated projects were developed. Some only exist in the form of concept art while others made it to the storyboarding stage. A few had some completed animation finished.

Some animated projects that were completed had segments eliminated like the famous "Dwarfs Eating Soup" sequence for *Snow White and the Seven Dwarfs* (1937) where Snow White tries to teach the little men to eat like gentlemen.

Walt decided to cut it even though it was ready to go to the Ink and Paint Department because he felt it slowed down the film at that point and distracted from the primary story. He did briefly consider making a sequel to the film that would have included this scene and another he cut about the Seven Dwarfs building a bed for Snow White.

Aladdin's mother was eliminated from the animated feature *Aladdin* (1992) because producer Jeffrey Katzenberg felt she added nothing to the story so it was decided to make Aladdin more sympathetic by being an orphan. It also meant the loss of an emotional song *Proud of Your Boy* written by Howard Ashman and Alan Menken where Aladdin sings about trying to become a better person for his mother. On the DVD extras, there is a deleted scene where both the mother and the genie urge Aladdin to tell Princess Jasmine the truth about himself. The song was so powerful that briefly it was even considered having Aladdin sing it to his dead mother in heaven.

The Los Angeles Daily News of July 26, 1992 stated:

> At a press preview for Disney's *Aladdin*, Disney studio chairman Jeffrey Katzenberg announced several animated feature projects in development (besides *King of the Jungle* due next year with songs by Elton John and Tim Rice). Those projects include *Homer's Odyssey, Sinbad the Sailor, Pocahontas, Swan Lake* (which Katzenberg described as "an original story dealing with the mythology of dragons)," *Song of the Sea* (about whales) and "a more lighthearted project" called *Silly Hillbillies on Mars*.

Only two of the films mentioned were ever produced, *Pocahontas* and *King of the Jungle* that had its title changed to *The Lion King*. The pre-production work on the other projects went back into the Disney animation vaults.

The little, mischievous black flying horse in the "Pastoral Symphony" segment of *Fantasia* (1940) was retroactively named Peter Pegasus by the Disney staff when he proved popular with audiences. Several Peter Pegasus shorts were planned and went into pre-production in the early 1940s, including one titled *Peter Pegasus* that would have been staged in a pantomime fashion to the music of Weber's *Invitation to Dance*. In the short he would have encountered the dancing mushrooms, another audience favorite from the "Nutcracker" segment of *Fantasia*.

The basic plot involved a series of misadventures after sneaking out of his nest, including following a family of ducks and trying to join them, and accidentally disturbing an angry bee while inspecting a flower which resulted in a battle in the air. It never progressed beyond the storyboard.

Not having a strong enough story was often the primary factor in not completing some of the proposed Disney animated projects. Both *The Little Mermaid* and *Beauty and the Beast* languished for decades because the studio could not find solutions to the story problems. However, money and lack of the necessary talent are also key factors as well.

Morgan's Ghost and Pirate's Gold (1941)

Mickey, Donald and Goofy appeared together in many memorable short cartoons including *Lonesome Ghosts* (1937) and *Mickey's Trailer* (1938). However, the trio didn't appear in a feature film together until *Fun and Fancy Free* (1947) with this variation of the "Jack and the Beanstalk" story providing some amusing and exciting moments. In truth, this adventure is more featurette length than feature length and had to be paired with another featurette *Bongo*.

Over the years, numerous ideas were submitted for a full length film featuring the three popular characters. To the best of my knowledge the very first full proposal utilizing the terrific trio in a full length movie was submitted October 21, 1939. Disney storymen Dick Creedon and Al Perkins wrote a typewritten proposal titled *Pieces of Eight or the Three Buccaneers*.

Creedon was credited as a writer on *Snow White and the Seven Dwarfs*. Carl Barks worked with Creedon on a story for the "proposed but never made" Mickey Mouse short cartoon, *Mickey of the Mounted* (August 1936). Perkins was credited as working on the *Reluctant Dragon* feature film.

The cartoon takes place at the Jolly Roger Inn in the old-fashioned water front village called Fish Haven. The inside of the inn is fitted out like the inside of a ship and along the walls are pictures of famous pirates. In the cage above the bar is a crotchety, salty parrot who entertains patrons with wild sailor yarns.

The Inn is operated by Mickey, Donald, Goofy and Pluto. They complain about the lack of patrons and the fact that they are dead broke. Suddenly, in a gust of wind and rain, Pete enters and is given food and drink. Other strangers arrive and sit with Pete and tell Mickey and the gang to leave them alone.

Mickey notices that each of the strangers looks like the famous pirates whose pictures are on the wall. They are the descendents of these famous villains. Eavesdropping, Mickey and his gang discover that the pirates each have a fragment of a treasure map. The villains grab the parrot and run off to their ship, The Vulture.

Mickey and the gang follow and disguise themselves as sailors to get abroad the ship to try and rescue their parrot. However, their disguises fool no one and they are kicked off the ship. Saying goodbye to Pluto (actually tying him up on the dock), Mickey, Goofy and Donald hide themselves in empty burlap bags and are hauled onto the ship. However, Pluto breaks free and chases the ship and at a bridge across the mouth of the harbor, jumps into the crow's nest with such force that he knocks himself out.

On board, Pete and his men torture the parrot "in some menacing but harmless way such as tickling him" and get the parrot to reveal the location of the treasure. The gathering is broken up by howls that the superstitious crew thinks might be the ghost of Robinson Crusoe on whose island the treasure is buried. It is Pluto stuck in the crow's nest. However, Pete is not fooled and chases Pluto into the hold where the pooch unwittingly reveals the hiding place of Mickey, Donald and Goofy.

The pirates decide to make the gang work for them during the voyage like peeling potatoes, swabbing the decks, etc. and then they will throw them to the sharks once they arrive at their destination. During the course of the voyage, Mickey and the gang have hidden a lifeboat, but when they attempt to escape they spill most of their supplies into the ocean.

The trio of friends along with Pluto face a number of misadventures on the lifeboat including mirages and near starvation. Eventually, the boat runs aground on the very island they have been looking for and they are rescued by lovely native dancing girls who fawn over them and feed them.

However, Mickey has not lost the reason for them being there, and with Pluto sets off into the mysterious jungle. They do find a treasure chest, but it is empty. They follow a winding path up to a stockade and poke around until they find where Crusoe has hidden the pirate treasure.

While Mickey and Pluto celebrate, Crusoe and his Man Friday arrive. In the distance, they hear jungle drums getting louder and using his telescope, Crusoe sees the natives marching Donald and Goofy up to the crater of a huge active volcano to sacrifice them. Mickey, Pluto and Crusoe rescue Donald and Goofy and take them back to the stockade.

Pete and his crew have discovered the empty treasure chest and have tracked Mickey to Crusoe's home. The villains mount an attack but Crusoe doesn't care whether they take the gold or not. It has no value to him on the island and he intends to stay on the island for the rest of his life. Mickey sparks Crusoe to action when he tells them that the pirates are holding Crusoe's beloved parrot as a hostage.

Crusoe's homemade defenses are pitted against machine guns, tear gas bombs and more. In the heat of the battle, Mickey vaults over the stockade to battle Captain Pete in hand-to-hand combat to rescue the parrot. This battle finally ends at the edge of the volcano crater with both combatants rolling over the edge toward the fiery lava below.

Pete's crew is turned over to the natives to be tossed into the volcano. Suddenly, a charred and ruffled parrot flies in to take everyone to the volcano where Mickey is not dead but hanging by the seat of his pants to a piece of lava sticking out from the side of the crater. With one hand, he hangs on to the rock and with the other he hangs on to Pete.

Mickey and Pete are pulled up to safety and the finale is Mickey and the gang sailing home with their ship full of treasure. All of the cut-throats are in chains doing the work on the ship. Crusoe who is newly re-united with his beloved parrot, waves good-bye to them from the shore.

Obviously, the popular novel *Treasure Island* provided a strong influence on the story proposal but as outlined by Creedon and Perkins the story offers some tremendous possibilities for gags and action.

Over the next two years, several storymen including Homer Brightman, Harry Reeves and Roy Williams reworked the idea and re-titled the story *Morgan's Ghost*. Nearly 800 storyboard drawings were attached to this new treatment, including an alternate ending as well as alternate gags for various scenes.

Mickey, Donald and Goofy are still the owners of a small tavern in a New England village called Fish Haven. On a stormy night, they are visited by a parrot with a peg leg named Yellow Beak. He is hiding from Black Pete because Yellow Beak has the treasure map of the pirate Henry Morgan. Yellow Beak offers to share the treasure if the trio can obtain a ship to get him to the island where the treasure is buried.

Pete overhears all of this discussion and disguises himself as an old woman and persuades the treasure hunters to lease his ship, the Sea Skunk. After a series of slapstick interludes at sea, Pete captures Yellow Beak and the map. He sets Mickey, Donald and Goofy adrift in a tiny raft. They wash ashore on a tropical island, the very one with the treasure.

They find an old chest that contains not gold but the nutty ghosts of Captain Henry Morgan and two of his crew. They have been trapped in the chest for a century and so they celebrate being released. They agree to help the trio rescue Yellow Beak and find the long lost treasure. The ghost of Captain Morgan can't tell the trio directly where the treasure is hidden because "Dead men tell no tales."

The trio and the ghosts rescue Yellow Beak and the map. A gap in the map has to be placed over the tattoo on Yellow Beak's chest to reveal the treasure's true hiding place. After battling man-eating plants, quicksand, and geysers, they find the gold.

There were actually two endings. One had Pete trying to take the loot but losing a game of "Who's Got the Drop on Whom?" with the good guys getting the treasure.

An alternate version has Pete taking the treasure and the down-hearted treasure hunters returning to their tavern. Their gloom is lifted when Donald bursts in with a newspaper and the headline that Pete has been arrested for passing counterfeit treasure.

Yellow Beak announces that he just remembered that what they found was a decoy treasure chest. The location of the real treasure is tattooed on his rear end!

Why did this feature never develop further? This story was being developed during the outbreak of World War II when feature animation projects were put on hold to concentrate all the Disney Studio efforts on work for the war from training films to Good Neighbor compilation films like *Saludos Amigos* as well as trying to keep up a series of theatrical shorts (many of which were also focused on war themes) with a reduced staff since many employees were serving in various branches of the Armed Services.

In the late 1930s and early 1940s, the Disney comic books being produced by Whitman/Western reprinted the Disney comic strips but by the mid-'40s the company was running out of material so it was decided to create original comic book stories featuring the Disney characters before the backlog of comic strips was completely depleted.

The West Coast editor of Western, Oskar LeBeck, was given permission to look through the Disney files of cartoon ideas that were shelved. He found the over 800 numbered sketches for *Morgan's Ghost* and was instantly struck that most of the work had already been done in terms of visualizing the story.

LeBeck felt it could easily be adapted into a Donald Duck comic book story substituting Donald's nephews for the Mickey and Goofy characters. Bob Karp, who was supplying gags for the Donald Duck comic strip at the time, was brought in to prepare a script based on the storyboards.

Karp took Photostats of the storyboards and re-scripted them for the comic book *Donald Duck Finds Pirate Gold* released in late 1942. Karp concentrated on the action sequences, limiting the dialogue in the final script.

He did make changes to make the story more consistent. Karp made some personal changes as well including changing Yellow Beak's desire for "sas" or sarsaparilla (a non-alcohoic drink similar to root beer) to "slumgullion" (a meat stew with vegetables) because it sounded more like something a pirate would want.

John Rose, who was head of the story artists for the animated shorts suggested Carl Barks and Jack Hannah as artists to illustrate the script into the final comic book story since they were the primary storymen producing the Donald Duck animated shorts. Not only storymen, Barks and Hannah were both talented cartoonists in their own right as well and were professional artists before they were hired at Disney.

Hannah recalled in an interview with me:

> A fellow named John Rose approached Carl and I and took us to meet Eleanor Packer who I believe was in charge of Whitman/ Western Publishing. They wanted us to draw 64 pages of a Donald Duck story. I suspect the reason we were chosen for this assignment was that it was a more story-related project.
>
> We were doing all the Donald Duck stories for the shorts and doing all the story sketches at the time so I'm just guessing that they probably felt we could work out this story as well, maybe even add in a few touches to help it flow properly or add a gag or two.
>
> We were given a typewritten script broken down into panels. The script had a brief scene description for each panel and, of course, the dialogue that needed to appear in that panel. It was left up to Carl and me on how to divide up the pages. I can't remember now how we decided to divide the thing up but I'm sure it made sense at the time.

Barks remembers the same situation:

> First, Bob Karp, who worked in the comic strip department, took Photostats of the storyboards, and from them he developed a typewritten script. That's why there's so little dialogue in *Pirate Gold*. Bob took it from the storyboards. In animation, they wanted things moving on the screen; they didn't want characters in held positions moving their lips.
>
> Jack and I never saw the storyboards. We were given the type-written script, broken down by panels. It would describe a ship or a dock or a room in some detail, to show what atmosphere should be developed in each panel. Then it would describe the action, like: 'Pete following a kid along dock—they go through a door.'
>
> We stuck to the script and didn't edit the material. Bob Karp was no dummy; he'd been writing the gags for the Donald Duck comic strips for many years. He was sharp on staging, and sharp on the amount of dialogue that was necessary. He wrote a good script. We were just beginners and assumed that we weren't allowed to do any tinkering.

Barks and Hannah divided up the drawing chores. Barks drew pages 1, 2, 5 and 12-40 with the rest being done by Hannah. In general, Barks drew the exterior scenes and Hannah the interior scenes.

Barks recalled:

We had a little talk together as to which pages we enjoyed or felt one of us could draw better than the other. We decided that I would take most of the outdoor scenes, the ones that showed the ship and its rigging … Jack took the indoor scenes. He had a wide knowledge of perspective and liked to draw shadow effects and furniture. … He took the ones he liked, and I took the ones I liked.

Barks used the May 1940 issue of *National Geographic* magazine for inspiration for the sea port town and the design of Black Pete's ship. Hannah recalled

At the time we were doing the comic book, neither Carl nor I had any idea that this was a proposal for a feature. It certainly seems strange that we never heard, because along with Jack King, we were directly responsible for all the Duck shorts coming out of the studio.

Still, if it were being developed as a feature, somebody may have felt it wasn't any of our business because we were just doing the shorts and this was a feature so it would involve an entirely different group of people. They certainly never told us. We were just given a typewritten script to work from and that was it.

We divided up the pages and worked on weekends and evenings. It was understood that the comic book work was not to be done on studio time. I'm guessing I penciled about a page and a half to two pages a weekend. We would draw it up in blue pencil and then it would have to be seen by the publishing company before we went ahead with the inking.

The inking went quicker than the penciling and I can't recall that there were any major changes we had to make on our blue pencil stuff. Carl and I had several meetings on the weekends so that the props we were drawing looked the same and that the room setting would be the same.

There would be the same pots on the stove or that kind of thing. We didn't have any difficulty synchronizing our style. We both fell into it easily and I think we were both surprised at how close the drawing was, especially since we were doing it in two different homes.

After all, when we did story sketches for the shorts, we had our own individual ways of drawing the story and both ways seemed to get the job done. Our art styles were a little different. So, in some ways, it was a real surprise to see the comic book work drawn so similar that it would be hard to tell which one of us drew the page.

We never did any of the actual work on the story at the studio. We may have discussed the story at the studio but I can't recall it so that probably means that type of discussion was infrequent at best.

The book was released in the Dell Four Color series. It was Four Color No. 9 entitled *Donald Duck Finds Pirate Gold* (October 1942). It was so popular that it began a series of original comic book stories featuring Donald Duck stories. Barks even left the Disney Studios and became one of the main writers and artists for the Disney duck comic book stories.

The story was similar to the proposed feature. Donald and his nephews are out trying to catch fish for the inn they run, Bucket O' Blood Sea Food Grotto, but a brewing storm robs them of their catch. A parrot named Yellow Beak appears for shelter and some slumgullion. Pete and his men track the parrot to the inn, but Donald and the boys hide Yellow Beak.

When Pete supposedly leaves, but actually remains outside to eavesdrop, Yellow Beak reveals that Captain Morgan's treasure map is hidden in the inn. When he retrieves it, he and the ducks make plans to get a ship the next morning and find the treasure. Pete has disguised his ship, Black Mariah, into the White Lily and Pete has disguised himself as a poor widow whose husband captained the ship but passed away two days ago so the ship is for sale cheap.

Yellow Beak buys the ship at the bargain price with the condition that the Widow Pete and her "brothers" are taken along as a crew. That night, Pete tries to locate the map and follows a sleepwalking duck nephew into the powder room and almost blows up the ship.

There are several comic misadventures on the ship including grabbing a Standard Oil Vacation Map by mistake. The truth about Pete and his crew is finally revealed and a comic chase ensues with Pete capturing Donald and Yellow Beak and making them walk the plank. The resourceful nephews have a waiting raft to save them and the heroes sail to the island while Pete and his crew find a vital part of the treasure map is missing.

When Donald and his group find the treasure chest in a cave, only one ghost claiming to be the ghost of Henry Morgan appears and gives them the rest of the map to locate the fortune.

Unfortunately, it is really Pete in disguise again using Donald and the nephews to use their part of the map to locate the treasure and dig it up which they do. However, Pete and his crew show up and get the drop on Donald and Yellow Beak. Thanks to the resourcefulness of the nephews, the crooks are rendered unconscious by coconuts.

The bad guys are taken back to the ship and chained up. While Donald and Yellow Beak argue over who is going to be the captain of the ship, the nephews have already taken over and are sailing into the sunset with the treasure.

In 1946, a condensed version of *Pirate Gold* was reprinted as *Donald Duck and Ghost Morgan's Treasure* in Better Little Book No. 1411. It was an *All Pictures Comics* book. Instead of the typical Big Little Book that had a page of text facing a page of illustration, this particular book had no text pages but all illustrations, including all the dialog balloons.

The panels from the original comic book were reformatted to fit the square panels in the book. Better Little Books were released by Whitman from 1938-1949 in an attempt to re-brand Big Little Books to compete with the explosion of comic books around the same time.

The same pirate tale with Yellow Beak, minus the Ducks, was recycled several times, as in Four-Color No. 227 (1949) in *The Seven Dwarfs* tale. A more elaborate version written by Del Connell for *Walt Disney's Peter Pan Treasure Chest No. 1* (January 1953) appeared as the story "Captain Hook and the Buried Treasure." It was illustrated by Dick Moores with Captain Hook substituting for Black Pete and the Peter Pan characters replacing the ducks.

Oddly, the story appeared yet again a decade later but this time in the non-Disney *Woody Woodpecker No. 76* (1963) comic also published by Whitman/Western, where Yellow Beak's appearance and name remained unchanged as he interacted with Woody. Disney comic book scholar Joe Torcivia discovered the unusual Woody Woodpecker version.

To earn extra money, Jack Hannah had done two Cheerios giveaway comic books in 1947. One of them was *Donald Duck and the Pirates* which was an interesting condensed variation re-telling of *Donald Duck Finds Pirate Gold*. It had a cover drawn by Carl Buettner but the artwork in the story is done by Hannah.

Donald and the boys are walking along the waterfront when in the alley they run across Yellow Beak, who has been attacked. They take him back to their house where Yellow Beak reveals his attackers were after his map to Captain Kidd's buried treasure.

Pete who was one of the attackers is outside and hears that Yellow Beak has a photographic mind and has taken a mental picture of the map. Donald and the boys decide to get a ship and accompany Yellow Beak to locate the treasure.

The next morning they see a sign on the side of a ship saying "For Sale. $8." However, when they pay the first mate the money, he laughs at their asking whether the ship is seaworthy.

The ducks think they have bought the ship but actually the sign was on a row boat hung on the side of the ship. Yellow Beak and the crew set sail, not suspecting that Pete and his cronies are the real crew on the ship and were sleeping down below.

The villains decide to hide so that they are taken to the treasure. While the ducks and Yellow Beak are sleeping, Pete grabs the parrot and puts him under an x-ray camera and takes a picture of his mental picture of the map.

Pete and his two henchman have the ducks and the parrot walk the plank but since they are so close to the island shore, they easily swim to land and in the moonlight search for the treasure.

Pete and his crew take the row boat to the island and then destroy it under the belief that the others won't be able to swim back to the ship with a treasure chest. However, he is wrong because the ducks have built a raft, load it with the treasure, row out to the ship and then sail the ship away while Pete and his cronies are left crying on the island.

There is a basic appeal to the story concept of *Pirate Gold* and it could still easily be revived as an animated feature vehicle for Mickey and his friends especially in the era of Captain Jack Sparrow and the Pirates of the Caribbean film franchise.

Donald Duck's Stratosphere Adventure (1939)

In an interview I did with storyman/animator/director Jack Hannah about his work on the Donald Duck cartoon shorts, he told me:

> I worked on a lot of cartoons, some with the Duck, that for one reason or another just never developed. A story may look like a good idea and then once you get into it, you just can't come up with enough gags or it would be too expensive to animate it correctly or just a lot of other things. It is important to know when to just stop and move on to something else.
>
> One of the most frustrating ones was this one Duck short where the Duck was working with a small elephant. It never made it to the screen.
>
> I thought we could do something with it in the animation. Norm Ferguson was assigned to me to do a lot of the animation and that became another problem. He wasn't able to do his best work because he was having some health problems. I think it was diabetes but he never said anything. I could immediately tell that he wasn't able to do what he used to do.
>
> I called Walt and said, "I've got this picture and it is just not coming together. I can't see what I could do to fix it. It would cost more money to fix it up than to junk it right now and start a new one."
>
> Walt said, "Well, if it's that bad, I agree with you." Walt always knew what was going on. He probably knew the picture was in trouble before I did. He knew that Fergie was having some problems and so that's why he didn't say anything else. I just threw the whole thing out and never saw it again.

In 1939, the story team of Carl Barks and Hannah worked on several Donald Duck shorts that didn't make it to the screen.

One of those shorts was *The Beaver Hunters* that had Donald and Pluto out hunting for beavers. Of course, the clever animals foil all their attempts. At one point Donald disguises himself as a tree and he also rigs his rifle to fire a plumber's helper plunger. Walt eventually felt that the personalities of the beavers were not appealing and the gags were flat.

Another short would have included Donald working in a museum and would have featured the parody paintings of Donald in classic paintings that were later featured in *Life* magazine (April 16, 1945). The colored sketches were actually done by Disney animators John Dunn, Phil Klein, and Ray Patin in 1939 as a gag during their free time, which is why they were available for consideration years before they appeared in the magazine.

Yet another Donald Duck story was titled *Donald's Stratosphere Flight* that would have detailed the problems Donald had with a hot air balloon, including launching and repairing it. It had originally been prepared as a Mickey Mouse cartoon story, with Mickey in a hot air balloon race with Pete, but it seemed it would be too complicated and expensive to produce and the whole concept of a race was removed.

Barks drew an inspirational sketch of Donald outfitted in full aviator gear for the project. Hannah told me:

> In 1939, I worked with Carl on a Duck cartoon called *Donald's Stratosphere Flight* where the Duck was going to set some new record going up in a hot air balloon. Actually we were told to design the cartoon so it could be easily animated by the new guys coming into the animation department.
>
> That meant to have some simple animation that didn't depend on personality to put across a gag. This was a way to train newer animators and give them some pencil footage experience.
>
> I don't remember how much time we spent on this story. I thought it had a lot of great possibilities but Dave Hand [director of *Snow White and the Seven Dwarfs* and Walt's right hand man at the time] never saw it as a priority. He was worried we were going to abandon working on *Donald's Vacation* [1940] which he really wanted to see.

Here is an excerpt from the story meeting on that short that Hannah gave me as a gift:

Story Meeting for Donald's Stratosphere Flight

Meeting Held: Monday, August 14, 1939. 9:30-10:30 a.m. Sweatbox No. 4

Those Present:

- Walt Disney
- Dave Hand
- Carl Barks
- Jack Hannah

(Carl Barks recapitulates story. Discussion opens.)

Walt Disney: Well, I'll tell you, I think it's the type of gag and the type of story that doesn't have a lot of subtle animation and things like that. I think it's worth developing, because that kind of gag will be easier to put over with less experienced men.

Dave Hand: Well, we would hold that idea there for future development. We would do nothing with it right this minute.

WD: Yes. You could just as well do away with the orchestra leader because your whole business there would be the anticipation of the balloon going up the minute they cut the ropes. That would take out some complications there.

The orchestra leader would fit in, but it's something that would sort of complicate the thing and it does take up a certain amount of footage. You could do the whole damn thing with just the three kids and the duck and leave out anyone else. It would simplify it. It seems like the whole idea would be strong enough without it.

DH: Even cutting out the grand stratosphere flight angle.

WD: That doesn't seem necessary at all. You plant the idea that it's a stratosphere flight just with this fancy looking balloon he has there and with the kids to send him off.

Carl Barks: It seems like with a crowd there it would be a better reason for him to make a success.

WD: When you analyze it, you have your audience sitting out there—he has to be a success to them.

Jack Hannah: Do you think we could do it with atmosphere.

WD: We always do that, but I wonder if we need it here. He is playing more or less to the audience that is sitting watching, because a lot of the effect you get anyway on the screen when things happen to the duck. He is sort of humiliated for the audience that is watching.

DH: That is true in *Good Scouts* and *Sea Scouts*.

CB: That is a subtle point, though.

WD: I don't know, but whatever you do I'd like to see you hold down a lot of that work there with crowds and things. Of course, it's possible you could take and pull it out of an old picture that we have already animated.

JH: It's easy to do—take one shot of old animation and plant it with your sound effects and band, etc.

WD: We even have a band that you could take out of the circus picture.

DH: In the *Tortoise and the Hare,* you have an opening like that.

WD: If you wanted to plant the band, you'd have to show shots and we have some stuff in that circus picture.

JH: If you can have the crowds without too much work, I think it would add something.

CB: That crowd in the *Tortoise and the Hare* picture is the best one.

WD: If the crowd is cheering him when he takes off and when he lands here in the middle of a barnyard and the cows are mooing and the chickens cackling, you could get the effect of a barnyard cheering that you could iris out on them cheering him. You can't get into these subtle gags until you know you have animators coming along to do them and this is good slapstick stuff. Not depreciating the business— you'll have to work to put this over with plenty of socko.

CB: The Duck never has an opportunity here to stand still long enough to let you see what he really looks like. Young guys could animate him swell.

WD: I think it's worth developing.

DH: Do you think in the point of variety and the possible need for footage because there isn't nearly enough footage here, that we might start out the picture with a sequence of the nephews filling up the balloon.

WD: What I'd do on that—you think there isn't enough footage, but we have always had trouble cutting out footage after a story goes into work and the director kicks that there is too much footage. So what the hell, let's go ahead and make a picture and build it in if we need it.

DH: In *Ice Hockey* we had to throw it back and add about 150 feet. It was because it was a fast-type picture.

WD: If that is the case, what you ought to do is get some simple type of stuff at the beginning.

CB: As Dave says, there might be some business in filling that darn balloon with gas.

DH: I meant a little sequence of gags there and then wipe right over to the big ascension and you're all ready to go.

WD: Where you could add footage, if you could make some kind of a speech at the beginning—you could just have an announcer there talking and "Donald Duck is going to reach the stratosphere!" and this and that so it builds up anticipation and "Donald Duck says, quote..." and you build it up big.

In other words, you can't have the Duck say it, but someone else is quoting the Duck. It gets comic with that announcer quoting the Duck. "I'll reach the thing or else—Wa-Wa-Wa!"

That is what you are building here—the guy gets such a hell of a big send off with what he is going to do. I saw a newsreel where a guy had these wings on and he had this whole suit on and he had an aviator's helmet on. I don't know whether it was a gag or not or whether the guy really thought he could fly.

The guy—no, it was a woman—and she'd give leaps and she couldn't get up and she couldn't get up and she kept giving these leaps and finally she came to a hill and jumped off and she fell flat on her puss. And God, it was a howl in the theater.

You get your audience feeling good and they are cheering this stratosphere flight, and the Chamber of Commerce comes in and puts this medal on him and, oh boy, is he proud of this medal and it's funny when he has to drop that medal overboard—it breaks his heart. We build it up there. He hates to do it.

DH: We work up the spirit of the thing.

WD: It's an easy thing to translate.

CB: When he comes to what the Duck says—where he quotes the Duck –would you try to make it sound like the Duck?

WD: You know what you could do before it happened, you could have both of the kids filling up the balloon and the announcer is talking and we cut inside to the Duck in there listening and, oh boy, he likes all this and he wants to make his grand entrance.

You have the Duck's reactions—you know he is a cocky little so and so. He loves this praise. You don't have to stay on announcer forever. The Duck comes out there and it's all set and ready and there ought to be a big ceremony to chopping the tie ropes. And Don is up there say-ing "Goodbye! Goodbye!" and he even kisses each one of the little kids goodbye, and then with much pathos, "Let her go!" and a big build up and then he doesn't go.

CB: That is kind of a subtle point to handle—it would require a lot of personality animation when the thing doesn't go up. That dumb look and the guy's disappointment.

WD: Wouldn't he close the whole damn thing, wouldn't he go inside and close the whole thing, and he is sitting in there waiting. "Well, well, I wonder where I am?" and he opens it up and looks down and there he is on the ground.

CB: He opens the door and makes a big gesture expecting to see the crowd way down on the ground.

WD: Maybe he gets a telescope and here is a bunch of ants crawling along the ground and he comes out with the telescope and he says they're so far away they look like ants and he looks through this thing and when he looks up here is everybody standing around looking at him.

CB: The audience could think he has gone up—that would be a laugh to them.

WD: They had another one of those things in a newsreel with a little lifeboat. [Here Walt explains the newsreel and the life boat invention.] There is some animation of a train in a trailer picture. Wherever you could use those things it saves that much. Even your smoke—there might be some smoke you could use. You can always cheat your set-ups around to use that stuff. I think this is a good gag type picture.

CB: There is an awful lot of gags that could come of that anchor rope. It might catch a factory whistle causing it to blow steam up on Don and the steam coming up there shrinks the balloon until it is only about four feet in circumference.

WD: It's good with Don ending up in a mud puddle with a bunch of pigs and the barnyard animals around there braying.

JH: The anchor might drag through a lake and catch a fish. There are so many set ups. You never have to stay with one thing.

WD: The medal idea is funny. I think it's worth working.

CB: How do you like that windmill stuff generally.

WD: That is all right. That is good stuff. There is nothing wrong with it, but I would watch for complicated things that would be hard to explain to an audience.

CB: You get a pattern up here of this thing going around and you see the pump rod moving up and down and the water coming out in sync with the pump rod, it explains the whole mechanism of the pump.

WD: The basket burning is funny. There is some good stuff in there with the Duck and it isn't complicated and your backgrounds are simple, and I feel it's the type of animation we can put over with the younger men, and we need work for them. That is the way we are going to get animators here. The more important stuff you could put a man on that could get it. What was your plan on this, Dave—just to keep developing it?

DH: If you like the basic idea, we'll just put it aside and when they finish up we can move this in. The Beaver picture is more developed than this and we can't work more than one thing at a time.

WD: Why don't they work on this as they have time?

DH: They will, but I just didn't want Jack to think that he was going to walk out on *Vacation,* because we want to see it.

WD: No, that is one thing we want to set our minds on. We want to build these stories until they are fool-proof. Really if we spent what we are supposed to spend on these pictures we are spending a lot of money, we should be able to do it or else we should get wise to ourselves and stop making them.

Forty-five thousand dollars is a lot of money to spend on a picture and it has to be a good picture to get that back, because by the time you put your print cost and your distribution cost on there, and other things that you have to contend with, and duty, and all that kind of stuff, that picture has to do $75,000-$80,000 to even clear itself, and there isn't one of these things that do even $50,000 gross.

So when we ask you to make a good picture for $45,000, it isn't unreasonable. It is poor economy on your part to start work on a story before it's ready and get it to where it costs a hell of a lot of money. Be sure we know the gag and be sure that it's workable. I think a lot of the time over there, the fellows just don't understand their gags. They have no definite workable plan in their mind to put a gag over.

I think a lot of this indecision has never been settled until after a thing is animated twice and then everybody gets together and figures it out. We just have to keep working on those stories. And now is the time to do it when it is in the story stage. Just make up your mind you're going to have to carry those through.

JH: I have to get in and time that thing for Leica and the rest of my crew have nothing to work on.

WD: We have to simplify it—for the sake of the gag you have to simplify it. I think we complicate gags a lot. There is no need of it. There is something about that skeleton of the Duck that is slightly repulsive.

CB: I saw it like an X-ray. Maybe that sketch is a little too vivid there.

DH: It might be better if you kept the Duck in half exposure instead of showing him all black.

WD: I don't quite get the X-ray connection.

CB: That is cartoon license, Walt.

WD: I think there has to be a certain amount of logic to it.

CB: I imagine if we didn't show his skull up here, he wouldn't look so gruesome. Just show his bones from the neck down. He'd look funnier without that death mask appearance. But there are probably funny things that could be done with electricity without the X-ray gag.

Danny Kaye's Weavie-Weavies (1944)

Walt Disney was always looking for other opportunities to help keep his studio solvent and find additional work for his artists. One solution was supplying short animated segments for other movie studios.

For instance, in the 20th Century Fox musical comedy starring actress Janet Gaynor, *Servant's Entrance* (1934), she is menaced during a roughly five minute dream sequence by kitchen utensils who put her on trial for her mistreatment of them. It included animation from the Disney Studio by Art Babbitt, Roy Williams, Woolie Reitherman, Jack Kinney and many other animators who would become legendary. Even Pinto Colvig, the voice of Goofy, supplies a voice for one of the animated characters.

In MGM's *Hollywood Party* (1934), a black and white segment with Mickey Mouse interacting with live action comedian Jimmy Durante introduces a Technicolor cartoon called *The Hot Chocolate Soldiers* that was reminiscent of the Silly Symphony series of the time. Mickey Mouse was largely animated by Fred Moore.

However, Walt produced an animated segment for another feature film that was completed but never included in the final release of the picture.

Up in Arms (1944) produced by Samuel Goldwyn and released through RKO marked the motion picture feature debut of Broadway and nightclub comedian Danny Kaye. The film was both a critical and a box-office hit, earning $3.3 million, and sparked Kaye's movie career.

Kaye played the part of Danny Weems, a hopeless hypochondriac who finds himself drafted into the army during World War II and shipped to a remote South Pacific island. The comic and romantic misadventures during the movie are just a loose framework to showcase Kaye's famous rapid-patter songs and natural comedic charm.

Unexpectedly, at the end of the film he becomes a hero by capturing a patrol of Japanese soldiers who are hiding on the island by dressing up and pretending to be their commander. The ending seems abrupt and even a little out of character for Weems who never previously demonstrated any heroism. There is also off screen narration to help audiences understand what is going on in the illogical story.

The reason for the confused ending may be because up until its release, that ending would have included an animation/live-action sequence produced by Walt Disney Studios and animated by Ub Iwerks.

As early as 1936, producer Samuel Goldwyn wanted to do a film about storyteller Hans Christian Andersen. By 1941, he had discussions with Walt Disney about producing animated segments of Andersen's famous stories (including one of *The Little Mermaid*) to include with the live action. The project fell through although Goldwyn later produced a similar film with Kaye as Andersen in 1952 but featured no animation.

Kaye was a longtime fan of Disney. Decades later, Kaye appeared as the host in the Smith-Hemion produced Disney television specials: *Kraft Salutes Disneyland's 25th Anniversary* (1980), *EPCOT Center: The Opening Celebration* (1982)

In the March 26, 1960 issue of *TV Guide* magazine, Kaye wrote:

> In the time of my grandparents, children were thrilled and chilled by Grimm's fairy tales, and grim they were and fairy tales they were also. The elders of the time certainly threw up their hands in horror at the violence of Grimm.

> Today, Walt Disney is heralded as one of the great storytellers of our time—which, indeed, he is. But what do we see with a Walt Disney film? We see horror and violence, after which good triumphs over evil. My daughter Dena had nightmares for a whole year after she saw *Snow White and the Seven Dwarfs*.

> I hold that neither Grimm nor Disney are the culminating factors in the definition of a child's personality. I think we would throw neither rocks nor puffs at them, but accept the fact that Grimm existed in his time and Disney does very well in our time.

The completed animation for *Up In Arms* was finished in black-and-white and ready for the final step of being done in color and combining it with the live action but at the last minute Goldwyn decided not to use it as he continued to make changes to the film. For instance, humorist Pete Smith had recorded the narration for the film but Goldwyn then had it re-recorded by Knox Manning.

In the case of the finale, Goldwyn felt the audience would feel cheated if they didn't see Kaye fighting the enemy on a cliff cave because the action in the original ending was obscured by strange, comical, animated insects called Weavie-Weavies literally eating the film away as it was being projected.

In an excited voice, the narrator would have described the great battle but the audience could only see only bits and pieces as the creatures kept eating away the images.

Goldwyn filmed a brief new ending with Kaye's character disguised as a general who leads the enemy soldiers into a pit. When Kaye trips the third soldier into his trap and he disappears, he lets out the famous Disney echoing "Goofy Holler" of "Wahoooey!"

The script describes the Weavie-Weavies as "animated caterpillar worms with almost human faces who appear from everywhere and start chewing holes in the film. As they eat chunks out of the film, we hear a sound like rabbits noisily chewing carrots."

They were to be a parody of the voracious appetite of Japanese silk worms who as larvae continuously eat mulberry leaves.

In the September 17, 1943 issue of the trade newspaper *The Hollywood Reporter,* it was announced that Disney was going to supply the animation for the sequence. An agreement had been made earlier on August 24, 1943 for Disney to do the work.

The Hollywood Reporter blurb stated:

> Samuel Goldwyn and Walt Disney announced yesterday that the Disney organization will do an animated sequence for *Up In Arms.* The sequence is already in work and will be presented as part of the climax of the film.

> They suspended work on their jointly proposed feature *The Life of Hans Christian Andersen* at the outbreak of the war, so that Disney could devote more of his time to production of films identified with the war effort and international relations. It is still on the Goldwyn-Disney agenda to be completed after the war.

An urban myth was that the Disney animation in the film would have featured the notorious gremlins popular during wartime that Walt had announced he was going to use in a feature film for RKO to distribute. That assumption is untrue. By March 1943, Walt had cancelled the plans to make the feature and by August 1943 had cancelled all plans to make an animated short subject with the gremlins as well.

In addition, Walt had to answer to writer Roald Dahl and the Royal Air Force who only wanted the gremlins used in reference to aircraft and, more particularly British aircraft, so would have been inappropriate for use in the Goldwyn film taking place in the South Pacific.

In November 1942, producer Cecil B. DeMille announced he was going to incorporate gremlins into a war related film he was developing but that never happened either.

A memo from Disney producer Harry Tytle to Avalon Productions dated September 14, 1943 for the production numbered 2679 had the following description for the ninety-seconds of animation that Disney would do on the sequence at the end of the film where Kaye was battling the Japanese soldiers:

SCENE 1: A medium long shot of Danny Kaye on a ledge. (Japanese soldier) is lowered by rope from left field. Weavie-Weavies crawl into film from off stage. Narrator explains their presence and yells "scram". Weavie-Weavies make a take towards camera and exit. (This setup is roughly shown by drawing No. 1)

SCENE 2: Would be close up of rope described above paragraph. (Japanese soldier) suspended from rope. Weavie-Weavie eats through film from reverse side and in large bites eats towards rope. We cut the scene when the Weavie-Weavie has eaten practically through the rope. Shown by sketches 2 and 3.

SCENE 3: Same setup as Scene 1. Approximately one foot after the start of scene, (Japanese soldier) who was suspended by rope falls from scene. Shown by sketch No. 4. This Weavie-Weavie disappears back of film. Another Weavie-Weavie eats cliff out from bottom of field as per sketch No. 5. Weavie-Weavie eats toward center as bottom Weavie-Weavie eats head and sword of (Japanese soldier). Weavie-Weavies continue eating around and part of action towards upper right hand corner.

Weavie-Weavies tug of war over last remaining bit of film. Film snaps. One Weavie-Weavie bounces off bottom portion of film and through hole that was previously eaten in film, screaming as he falls off stage.

Remaining Weavie-Weavie looks down and offstage as he hears long scream or yell. Shown by sketches No. 6 through No. 12.

SCENE 4: Close up of Weavie-Weavie as he turns towards audience and goes through dialogue: "Now you'll never know what happened! I'm the only one who knows and I'll never tell! Never, never, never!" Cut. Shown by drawings No. 14 and 15.

The memo continued:

> We do not wish to be held to the exact letter as we will probably take certain liberties with this proposed draft. We are proceeding with this outline. If they object, we suggest they get in touch with us immediately as we are trying to move the production as fast as possible at their request.

Both Ub Iwerks and animator George Nicholas who was working on the Pluto shorts were copied on this information. Iwerks later directed the sequence and did most if not all of the animation. The following year Iwerks would develop a process for combining live action and animation for *The Three Caballeros*.

On Friday September 10, 1943, Avalon Productions delivered to the Disney Studio prints of the live action from *Up In Arms* and viewed the animation test that was met with approval.

The Disney Studio then moved the scene through to a final production with some minor changes of its own. It was determined that the delivery date for the final work would be October 11, 1943, roughly three weeks later.

On October 21, 1943, Disney Studio lawyer Gunther Lessing wrote to reaffirm a phone conversation that giving Disney credit for the cartoon sequence was optional to the company even though it had been required in the original agreement.

Scott McQueen, former senior manager of film restoration for the Disney Company, used to travel around the country with a program of Disney film rarities that he had unearthed entitled "Disney's Unseen Treasures."

He did the presentation at the Disney Institute on January 25, 1997 which is where I saw it and talked with McQueen after the show. In the presentation, he included the complete segment he had found from the *Up In Arms* film.

There was live action color footage of Kaye doing hand-to-hand combat with the Japanese soldiers outside a cave on the side of the mountain with black-and-white animation layered over the top where the little creatures (who had several hands/legs, two antenna and a point on the end of their bodies like a stinger) poke into the picture and literally eat up the screen including a rope hanging down on the left side of the mountain causing a soldier who was hanging on to fall to his doom.

The final image has of one of these little caterpillars finishing off a final bite and then looking at and talking extensively to the audience in a close-up. He ends with a huge laugh and then belches loudly and wiggles off the screen.

The inside of his mouth is painted a bright red but there was no other color on the creature. McQueen could not locate the dialog script or the sound track for the segment.

The face of the Weavie-Weavies is very reminiscent of 1930s Disney characters like Bucky Bug.

At first the narrator blames the disintegrating film perhaps on a type of mildew indigenous to tropical climates but then offers the explanation that it is perhaps an unusual South Seas pest known as "Weavie-Weavies".

During the battle, the script has the narrator panicking: "Ooooooh! I'm sorry folks. It's those Weavie-Weavies again! Can't seem to keep them off the film! Get off of there, you worms! Folks, if you look carefully you can still see some of the fight going on!"

So locked in its vaults, Disney has the completed animation for the segment but not the final Technicolor version which was probably not finished.

As an independent producer, Goldwyn had been fighting against theater chain monopolies that were operated by the big studios and offered smaller rental fees to independents. The theater chain owner in Reno, Nevada offered Goldwyn a flat film rental fee for *Up In Arms*.

Goldwyn responded by converting the El Patio ballroom outside the city into a makeshift theater at his own expense and pledged to donate the opening night box-office to the local chapter of the Red Cross. Goldwyn was a member of the Society of Motion Picture Producers (SIMPP) along with Mary Pickford and Walt Disney.

Pickford showed up opening night to give a speech in support of Goldwyn and all independent producers. She read a letter written by Walt Disney who also supported the situation. The publicity drew national attention.

There was one more encounter between Disney and Goldwyn.

Some readers may be familiar with the Samuel Goldwyn film with Danny Kaye entitled *A Song Is Born* (1948), which was a remake of the Gary Cooper/Barbara Stanwyck screwball comedy *Ball of Fire* (1941). Both films were directed by Howard Hawks and produced by Goldwyn.

Goldwyn originally wanted the film to be a sort of live action version of Disney's *Snow White and the Seven Dwarfs*. Basically, the storyline is seven quirky bachelor music professors (plus the Cooper/Kaye character who is supposed to be the prince who rescues the damsel in distress) working on an encyclopedia of music.

They have their comfortable lives invaded by a hard-edged female who is hiding out from the authorities and is the girlfriend of a wanted gangster. She introduces them to popular music since their expertise is just classical music.

For *Ball of Fire*, the publicity department staged a portrait of the seven actors playing the professors seated in front of a poster for *Snow White and the Seven Dwarfs*, with each in the same position as the dwarf he represented: S.Z. Sakall (Dopey); Leonid Kinskey (Sneezy); Richard Haydn (Bashful); Henry Travers (Sleepy); Aubrey Mather (Happy); Tully Marshall (Grumpy); and Oskar Homolka (Doc).

"It actually was *Snow White and the Seven Dwarfs*—with the striptease dancer as Snow White," said Hawks in the book *Who the Devil Made It: Conversations With Legendary Film Directors* by Peter Bogdanovich.

For *A Song Is Born*, Goldwyn went so far as to correspond with Disney to get permission to use the *Heigh Ho* song from the Disney film. Disney denied permission and other direct references to the Seven Dwarfs were eliminated as a host of un-credited writers tried to rework the original screenplay.

The Roger Rabbit Prequels (1992)

Who Framed Roger Rabbit (1988) revived the general public's interest in animation, introduced several memorable new animated characters, was a goldmine in merchandise, and spurred ill-conceived projects from other studios attempting to duplicate its success in combining live-action and animated characters.

Originally budgeted at around $12 million in the early 1980s, the film finally came in with a cost estimated at close to $50 million. Reviews were generally mixed but positive. Reviewers were astounded by the technology, but found story and character deficiencies.

The film toppled almost every Disney financial record. *Roger* broke theater records around the world. It became the top-grossing film that year (more than $150 million in the United States alone and $325 million worldwide on its first release), and one of the top money-making features of all time.

The feature received a number of prominent award nominations. The Golden Globes nominated it for Best Picture and Best Actor (Bob Hoskins). The script was nominated for best script based on material from another medium by the Writers Guild of America.

The Directors Guild nominated Robert Zemeckis for best director. Even Charles Fleischer, the voice of Roger, was nominated for best supporting male by the American Comedy Awards for his role.

Though it didn't win any of these awards, this was a sign of how well-received the film was in the professional community. Other award recognition included a Hugo award and a Kids Choice award.

Roger did well at the Oscars. Nominated in a number of categories, it went on to win three Oscars for its technical work (Best Sound Editing, Best Visual Effects, and Best Film Editing). Additionally, an Honorary Oscar for special achievement went to Richard Williams "for animation direction and creation of the cartoon characters."

An animated Roger was scheduled to appear at the Oscar ceremonies, but last-minute production problems prevented it from happening.

However, to save money on what was initially considered an expensive and risky production (it was purposely released under the Touchstone Pictures label not Disney), Disney CEO Michael Eisner suggested that Disney and Spielberg's Amblin studio co-produce the film and share the uncertainty.

Eisner was thinking about the previous Disney partnership with Paramount Studios for the 1980 live action *Popeye* film that had been written off as a flop because it was not a blockbuster or generated a franchise.

Eisner was also counting on Spielberg to be able to persuade other studios to allow their characters to be used in a Disney film and, in fact, Spielberg was able to negotiate the rights to many animation icons with some stipulations for only $5,000 for each character.

However, Spielberg insisted that Amblin and Disney would share the copyright on any new characters created for the film like Roger, Jessica, Baby Herman and Benny the Cab. In addition, the two studios would split evenly the profits from the film and any merchandise. Finally, both parties would have to agree on any future project using the characters.

After the release of the film, Disney immediately started featuring Roger in the Disney theme parks, ramped up a plethora of merchandise, and green-lit a sequel film feature.

Unfortunately, because of the production necessities of the time, the earliest a sequel could appear would be in 1992, and perhaps later, since Zemeckis had already gone on to simultaneously direct the two sequels to his film *Back to the Future* (1985) that would be released in 1989 and 1990.

In the *New York Times* April 19, 1990, Peter Schneider, then senior vice president of Disney feature animation said:

> Keeping Roger Rabbit alive has proven to be a challenge since the sequel isn't expected to open in theaters until summer of 1992. Roger is the first time in many years that a cartoon character has come off of a movie and become a character audiences want to see more of.
>
> Once we saw he really did transcend the movie, the question was how to keep him alive. Of course, there is merchandise but the key to longevity is the screen which is why we are doing theatrical shorts.
>
> However, shorts these days are almost as complicated to make as a feature film. We look at it both ways. They are as complex as a feature but at the same time six minutes is definitely easier to do than seventy minutes so, of course, it's easier to manage. It's also a great way to try out new people, train them for the features.

A continuing series of shorts were agreed to by Spielberg in order to keep the characters in the minds of the audience and build anticipation for the upcoming sequel.

Voice artists Charles Fleischer (Roger), Kathleen Turner (Jessica), Lou Hirsch (adult Baby Herman), and April Winchell (Mrs. Herman), returned to reprise their roles from the original film.

In addition, from the original film, producers Steven Spielberg, Kathleen Kennedy, Frank Marshall, and Don Hahn were attached. Marshall would also direct the live-action segments in the first two shorts.

Don Hahn told writer Desmond Ryan for a June 25, 1989, article:

> I worked on Roger Rabbit for two and a half years so I know,. The earliest we could hope to have a sequel out with the way things are is 1992. There are many factors. One of them is, while we've figured out how to do combining live action and animation, we would want to top the first one.
>
> Roger has been so successful that we're in a position where a cartoon short can help a movie from a marketing standpoint. There's a tremendous value for us in keeping the characters alive. Roger is everywhere right now, and we want to make sure it stays that way. This [making theatrical shorts] is the best way to do it until the second feature.

Producing these shorts would also provide work for the new Disney satellite animation studio that opened in Orlando, Florida at Disney MGM Studios.

Just as attaching the first new short *Tummy Trouble* to Disney's *Honey, I Shrunk the Kids* helped that film's box office, Spielberg wanted the second short *Roller Coaster Rabbit* (1990) to be attached to his Amblin film *Arachnophobia* that was being produced for Disney's new Hollywood Pictures division.

However, Eisner was worried about the success of the upcoming, big budget *Dick Tracy* film being produced by Disney and felt the short could help its box office take more than the Amblin film.

Since both films were being released by Disney, Eisner made the final decision to put the new Roger Rabbit short with *Dick Tracy*. It was felt in the entertainment industry that so doing did help the film, but that it would have helped *Arachnophobia* do better if it had been attached to it instead.

Spielberg felt he was being disrespected and that his co-ownership rights were being ignored. Disney had begun production on the next Roger short, *Hare in My Soup,* when Spielberg announced he didn't like the story and demanded production be shut down. Disney pitched several other ideas but Spielberg rejected all of them for roughly two years.

He eventually approved *Trail Mix-Up,* which had originally been planned to be attached to *The Rocketeer* (1991), but couldn't meet the deadline. It was attached to a Disney/Amblin co-production, *A Far Off Place (1993).*

Several Roger Rabbit shorts were announced as in development but were never completed: *Hare in My Soup, Clean and Oppressed, Beach Blanket Bay,* and *Bronco Bustin' Bunny.*

Hare in My Soup would have taken place in a restaurant and, when Mrs. Herman goes to powder her nose, Baby Herman wanders off into the kitchen. Chaos ensues. Roger would have been a clumsy waiter once again struggling to save Baby Herman from harm.

For a feature film follow-up to the original film, the first idea was written by Nat Mauldin (son of famous Pulitzer-award-winning World War II cartoonist Bill Mauldin). It would be a prequel entitled *Roger Rabbit: The Toon Platoon.*

It was set during World War II and would have shown how Roger met Jessica when she was working at a radio station in Hollywood. Roger had come to Hollywood in search of his birth mother.

Mauldin had some impressive television comedy credits, including *Barney Miller* and *Night Court,* and would later write screenplays including Eddie Murphy's *Dr. Dolittle* (1998) and the computer animated feature *Open Season* (2006). Obviously, his father's experiences in World War II influenced the screenplay.

Jessica works at a radio studio doing sound effects and is kidnapped by the station manager, who is a Nazi spy. She is taken to Nazi Germany to do propaganda broadcasts like Tokyo Rose and Axis Sally did during the conflict.

Roger recruits his fellow toons who are serving in Europe, including Swifty Turtle and Blackie Cat, to go and rescue her. The major revelation at the end would be that Bugs Bunny was Roger's father.

Since Roger hadn't met Eddie Valiant yet, a new live-action human companion was created in Richie Davenport, an aspiring young actor going to Hollywood who later enlists and is assigned to a supply base run by toons, because his fear of heights endangered his original troop.

Jessica's roommate is a live-action human named Wendy and she is also kidnapped. Richie falls in love with Wendy, and he overcomes his fears to help rescue her.

However, Spielberg had gone through a personal revelation after directing 1993's *Schindler's List* and felt that comedic portrayals of Nazis were disrespectful to the victims of the Holocaust, so he rejected the premise. He stated he wanted to avoid using Nazis as villains in his future films, yet ended up doing so in 1998's *Saving Private Ryan.*

New scriptwriters Sherri Stoner and Deanna Oliver, who had worked on other Spielberg animation projects, including the *Tiny Toons* and *Animaniacs* series were brought in and changed the setting from Hollywood to New York City during the Great Depression. The film was now re-titled *Who Discovered Roger Rabbit?*

It was still a prequel to the original film, but this time Roger, who was raised by a human couple in the Midwest, discovers he is actually a toon and goes on a journey to find his real mother. He takes the journey to New York and Broadway.

On Broadway Jessica is appearing in a show where Roger gets a job backstage. His slapstick antics as a stagehand results in him ending up on stage and becoming a comedy star when the audience falls in love with his physical comedy. He is soon offered a job in Hollywood movies.

The character of Richie Davenport as an aspiring actor is retained from the first version, and it was rumored that actor Tom Cruise might play the role. He is Roger's vaudeville partner doing a "magician and his rabbit in the hat" routine and is considered the one with real talent until Roger's unexpected break.

The film was meant to be a loving tribute to RKO and MGM Hollywood musicals of that same period and composer Alan Menken was so enthused by the script that he wrote five songs for the project with lyrics by Glenn Slater. Menken even offered to executive produce the film. One of the songs was *This Only Happens In the Movies*.

Lyricist Slater told writer Jeremie Noyer of *Animated Views* in 2008:

> *This Only Happens in the Movies* was written for one of the early scenes in the film. Roger and his friend have just arrived in Hollywood, and have been hired as waiters at a grand party thrown by the town's biggest producer, to celebrate his new movie musical, starring a celebrated Fred Astaire/Ginger Rogers-type dancing duo.
>
> After toasting the stars of the film, the producer asks them to perform one of their famous numbers, called *This Only Happens in the Movies*. The male half of the team, a nasty drunk, is too incapacitated to perform; but Roger's friend, who has had a long-time crush on the female star, steps forward and says that, having seen every one of the team's previous films dozens of times, he has memorized the entire routine and can step in for the star.
>
> The female half of the team is skeptical, but the crowd insists. They begin to perform the number, dutifully singing the words to the old song; but Roger's friend is truly good—better than the star himself—and as they sing the words, about the kind of moments that are so perfect they can only happen in movies, they begin to have one of those moments themselves.
>
> By the end of the song, they have begun to live the song, and have fallen in love 'at first sight', just like in a corny old Hollywood musical. And as the song ends, as they gaze into each other's eyes and the crowd holds its breath, of course Roger destroys the mo-

ment by accidentally causing a catastrophe of broken dishes, fly-ing cutlery and general mayhem.

The idea was to create a shimmering beautiful moment for Roger to utterly and completely ruin, so the song needed to be, in a sense, the very opposite of what you would associate with Roger Rabbit.

We wrote a song for Jessica called *Good Little Girl*. In the script, Jessica is a former child star, with a stage mother who insists that she keep singing her old songs and wearing her old costumes. Needless to say, the old costumes fit rather differently now that Jessica has, uh, blossomed into womanhood.

And the old songs, which would have sounded very innocent coming from a young girl, now have a very different effect with lyrics that are one double-entendre after another.

There was another song, called *Things Like Us Don't Happen Every Day*, that we made a demo for, but I don't remember how it fit into the film. And then there were a few other half-finished numbers.

Jim Pentecost who produced *Pocahontas (1995)* would have pro-duced, but Eisner was worried about the budget so a ten second an-imation "pitch test" was directed in spring 1998 by animator Eric Goldberg in Florida.

Goldberg drew up a model sheet for a younger (and simpler to draw) Roger and did a 2-D version (characters were hand drawn, but all props they interacted with were CGI) and also a 3-D version utilizing all CGI including for the characters.

Goldberg had been tapped to be the animation director for the proposed sequel, taking over the role that Richard Williams had in the feature.

As Goldberg explained:

Whether we would use the technique or not in the sequel, it was to prove that we could do Disney quality animation in CGI, which no one had ever attempted before. The Florida team proved me right, in spades, and major kudos to them all.

The next logical step for the studio was to see if we could achieve that kind of animation without pre-animating it as 2-D first. The result was Magic Lamp Theater, now a popular 3-D stereo attrac-tion at Tokyo DisneySea.

The first test had two hand-drawn animated weasels busting into the live-action office of a Hollywood agent and using their CGI tommy guns to threaten him to audition Roger.

Roger, who was also hand drawn bursts in, jumps on a table to dance and causes havoc, including scattering the objects on the agent's desk.

The second test done completely in CGI was the one Eisner liked the best but he did not like the projected cost, an estimated one hundred million dollars nor that the studio had lost money on some recent sequels. In the summer of 1999, Eisner suspended all pre-production.

The money that would have gone to the sequel was invested in the film *Pearl Harbor* (2001). That film was budgeted at $208 million dollars and brought in $200 million domestically.

There were several reasons for the sequel never being made, besides Eisner's feeling that it would be much too expensive an investment. The concern was other studios would now want more money for the use of their characters and too much time had passed from the original film so there was no momentum, as well as the challenges of working with Spielberg.

Eisner had assumed that Spielberg would just rubber stamp all decisions about the characters and, when that didn't happen, it raised a major red flag. In addition, Eisner saw half the money from Roger Rabbit leaving the Disney Company to go to Spielberg. It was something that personally irritated him.

Eisner wrote:

> By the time it [the original film] premiered, we had licensing agreements for over 500 products, ranging from Jessica Rabbit jewelry to Roger Rabbit talking dolls to computer games. Both McDonald's and Coca-Cola created massive promotional tie-ins.

Of course, Eisner had not had much faith in the original film while it was being made, which is why he made the deal with Spielberg in the first place and released the film under the Touchstone label. Today, it is officially considered a Disney film like the animated classics.

Eisner felt he had wisely hedged his bets by doing it as a co-production that would minimize any Disney losses and, according to his autobiography, "we had hoped to distance it [the film] from the Disney brand by releasing it under the Touchstone label."

At Disney, there was the real fear that the film might turn out to be another *Howard the Duck* (1986) box office disaster (a comic book character in a human environment) or even a public relations nightmare because of some of the controversial elements in the film that Eisner considered "too sophisticated and sexy."

Eisner pulled Roger Rabbit from the Disney theme parks, ceased production on the massive amount of Roger Rabbit related merchandise and cancelled plans for a Roger Rabbit section for both Disneyland and Disney-MGM Studios theme parks.

Artist Peter Emsile remembered that he had just completed the image of Roger Rabbit for the WDW 20th Anniversary press kit cover when word came from Eisner to stop any and all projects that featured Roger. So, 1992 was the end of the massive promotion of Roger Rabbit and his friends by Disney although some projects that had been started were completed.

Disney tried unsuccessfully to create their own Roger doppelganger with an animated character called Bonkers D. Bobcat. Bonkers was a hyperactive anthropomorphic bobcat who worked in the Toon Division of the Hollywood police department after his movie career ended at Wackytoons Studio.

The character appeared in the Walt Disney Television syndicated animation series *Disney's Raw Toonage* (1992) and *Bonkers* (1993).

He failed to capture either the affection of the audience or the plaudits of the critics. He was seen as what he truly was: an attempt to create another Roger Rabbit character with no connections to Spielberg and going "on the cheap," without using the combination of live-action and animation. In the series, humans were animated drawings, as well.

Another reason for concern about the sequel was that former Disney Studio executive Jeffrey Katzenberg had left Disney on bad terms and was now partnered with Spielberg at Dreamworks SKG working on animated features.

Eisner felt that Katzenberg for revenge might sabotage any Roger Rabbit feature film sequel, so he made two former Amblin producers who Spielberg liked and respected, Frank Marshall and Kathleen Kennedy, producers of the proposed film. Spielberg quietly acceded to pre-production work continuing on the project in order to give his two friends and former co-workers their shot at producing.

In 2013, working with producer Erik Von Wodtke, Gary Wolf, author of the original novel *Who Censored Roger Rabbit* (1981), pitched three ideas for Roger Rabbit shorts and a Roger Rabbit feature to Disney.

The shorts included two written by Von Wodtke and Wolf: *Rear Window Rabbit* (a parody of the Alfred Hitchcock film *Rear Window*) and *The Birds* (another parody of a famous Hitchcock film but featuring Disney birds). In addition, Wolf wrote a short entitled *Roger Rabbit Returns*.

Wolf also pitched an all-animated feature film for Roger Rabbit called *The Stooge* inspired by the 1952 Dean Martin and Jerry Lewis movie but not a direct remake.

Wolf told me:

> It stars Mickey Mouse and Roger and is set to take place throughout five specific locations in Disneyland park and will also bring both Walt Disney and Orson Welles back to life via motion-capture.

In November 2016, director Zemeckis, after years of vacillating back and forth, said he was still interested in doing a sequel, but felt that Disney had no interest.

Zemeckis had another script for the sequel by writers Jeffrey Price and Peter Seaman that he felt was "magnificent" and would "follow up from the world of film noir in 1947 to the next few years of the 1950s. It is more a continuation than a sequel. Rather than recasting Bob Hoskins (who died in 2014), we would include a digital version."

Zemeckis alluded to the story point that the character of Eddie Valiant would be a ghost, and perhaps use motion capture to achieve the effect and perhaps on other characters, as well.

He stated:

> The current corporate Disney culture has no interest in Roger, and they certainly don't like Jessica at all. Most sequels, you're behind the eight-ball on them. Audiences want it to be the same movie, but different. If it's too similar, they don't like it. And if it's too different, they really don't like it. There's nothing more difficult.

Zemeckis had submitted an early draft of the script to Disney in 2012 and got no response. At one point even producer and director J.J. Abrams worked on a possible sequel.

Producer Don Hahn has said the project should remain dead because the public's taste in animation has changed significantly since the original feature film was released and the market has been flooded with animation.

"There was something very special about that time when animation was not as much in the forefront as it is now," he replied when asked about reviving the idea of a sequel.

Hiawatha (1949)

The Song of Hiawatha is a famous 1855 epic poem written by Henry Wadsworth Longfellow about the fictional adventures of an Indian warrior named Hiawatha based on Native American legends.

In the poem, Hiawatha has many childhood adventures, falls in love with the beautiful Minnehaha (who later dies), defeats an evil magician named Pearl-Feather, invents written language, discovers corn and many other dramatic episodes. It was instantly popular and became highly influential over the decades.

Walt Disney first encounted the poem when he was a student at Benton Elementary School in Marceline, Missouri through one of the editions of the McGuffey Eclectic Readers series that featured excerpts from the works of what were considered great writers.

Walt had a great respect for Native American culture. His wife, Lillian, had grown up in Lapwai, Idaho, on the Nez Perce Indian Reservation where her father worked for the government as a black-smith and federal marshal. Her mother would regale Walt with stories of real Indians she had personally encountered.

Even Walt Disney's popular Davy Crockett television series treated Native Americans with greater respect and affection than other producers of the time period. Crockett spends much of the series helping and defending Native Americans.

Nearly 200 of the Native Americans that appear in the series were actual Cherokees. This was quite a change from the typical Hollywood productions that were casting Italians and Hispanics as Native Americans.

When Disneyland opened in 1955, Walt had an Indian Village in Frontierland that celebrated Native American culture and was in stark contrast to the portrayal of Indians in television shows and movies that were popular at the time.

Disney did produce the Silly Symphony *Little Hiawatha* in May 1937 which was about the misadventures of a typical "cute" little kid whose pants kept falling down. He paddled his canoe deep into the forest to go hunting.

He had to be saved from an angry bear by the animals he had been too softhearted to kill. The story has no real connection to the epic poem and the title was simply chosen for its name recognition by an audience just as it was by other cartoon studios. It might be considered a parody of the Native American "mighty hunter" of Longfellow's tale.

The Disney character was popular enough to be considered for a sequel where he would meet Little Minnehaha designed by artist Walt Kelly of *Pogo* fame. Little Hiawatha appeared in the Silly Symphony Sunday newspaper comic strip from November 10, 1940 to July 12, 1942. Later, he appeared in several stories in *Walt Disney's Comics & Stories* published by Dell Comics as well as four single issues of *Dell's Four Color* comic series.

However, Walt had bigger plans in mind for the story of Hiawatha. In 1940, storyman Ted Sears worked up a serious cartoon short entitled *Pipe of Peace* where Hiawatha playing his flute brought peace between all the animals and humans.

As animators Frank Thomas and Ollie Johnson wrote in their book *Disney Animation: The Illusion of Life*:

> Walt was always way ahead of any of us, searching for new procedures, new forms of entertainment. One theme that kept haunting him was the story of Hiawatha. He kept bringing it up over the years, trying to find the right way to do something with it.
>
> He said to us, "There's something there, y'know? Something we could do—something that's right for us. I don't know what it is or how we'd do it. Don't think of a film, don't even think of a show—don't limit your thinking to a regular theater. Maybe it's something out in the woods, or on a mountain, maybe the people are brought in—or—I don't know—but there's something there!" He felt the subject needed something beyond a film to be properly presented.

Author Bob Thomas wrote in *Walt Disney: An American Original*:

> Walt had an instinct for recognizing when the film project was not going well. Sometimes there were stories that defied solution and he simply dropped them (like *The Little Mermaid* and *Beauty and the Beast*). Months, perhaps years later, he picked up the project and started all over again. By this time, his creative conscious may have provided a solution.
>
> A Hiawatha feature metamorphosed over a period of twenty years and when a story man lacked an assignment, Walt instructed, 'Put him on *Hiawatha*'. But, despite all the efforts, *Hiawatha* was never produced.

In 1943, Walt seriously started work on Hiawatha as a feature film. At one point, he considered having Native American artists do concept art and to employ it in some way in the finished film.

Starting in animation, Dick Kelsey became an art director at the studio on *Pinocchio* (1940), *Fantasia* ("Rite of Spring segment) (1940), *Dumbo* (1941), and *Bambi* (1942). By January of 1943, Dick Kelsey had traded in that title at the studio for Lieutenant in the U.S. Marines. Between 1943 and 1945, Kelsey would not only be promoted to Captain of the Division, but also supervised a relief map unit.

On his return to the studio, Walt had a special assignment for him. He put him in charge of a crew of artists to create storyboards for the proposed Hiawatha animated feature. In 1948 and 1949, Kelsey almost single-handedly produced an impressive number of atmospheric storyboards.

They were so evocative and accurate that decades later they were pulled out of storage to be studied for the Disney animated feature *Pocahontas* (1995). The research on historic costuming and background material had been impressive.

The New York Times for May 25, 1948, headlined "Disney Set To Film Story on Hiawatha; Feature Length Cartoon Devised Without Live Action."

From an Associated Press newspaper account dated September 12, 1948:

> Dick Kelsey, one of Disney chief staff artists will spend six weeks (starting Sept 25) touring the Great Lakes Region sketching and documenting the settings of Longfellow s famous narrative poem.
>
> His Itinerary includes Chicago, Minneapolis-St. Paul, the shores of Lake Superior and Michigan, Ann Arbor, Lansing and Detroit across Lake Erie to Buffalo then through Rochester the Finger Lakes district the Mohawk Valley down the Hudson to New York and on to Washington for museum data. Color camera records will supplement his sketches.
>
> The finished cartoon likewise will be in color. Kelsey's will be no easy task in this modern era since he insists he will try to recapture both the spirit and the look of Hiawatha's land. Every remaining forest, prairie, lake and river associated with the Indian legend will be visited by boat, automobile, train, horse or on foot, he declared.
>
> He has arranged to study museum material in Chicago, St Paul, Minneapolis, and Rochester, the American Museum of Natural History and the Heye Foundation in New York and the Smithsonian Institute and the Bureau of Indian Affairs in Washington. At Naples, NY he will confer with Dr. Arthur C. Parker, director emeritus of the Rochester Museum, an authority on American Indian life and lore.

The story kept evolving as Walt sought to condense the sprawling poem into a story that could be told within the confines of a single film. At one point, Walt even considered having the characters deliver their lines in sign language and so research was done at the Smithsonian Institution but was abandoned as the story became too complicated to tell in that fashion.

An early version of the story started with an inter-tribal war and the Great Spirit sending a deliverer in the form of Hiawatha to re-establish the peace and prosperity. Disney storymen added a villain named Tadodaho who was a feared warrior and whose jealousy of Hiawatha results in various acts of treachery including killing Hiawatha's best friend. Eventually the villain dies in a massive snow storm and Hiawatha is vindicated from all the earlier actions Tadodaho took to undermine Hiawatha in front of the tribe.

Kelsey told the other artists at the studio:

> Walt doesn't want to make this a light thing...he wants it [to have] a terrific musical accompaniment—almost Christ-like but not quite...Walt said it was originally his idea to get the storyboards up to show the material we are going to work with, then call in the composer—tell the story like we just told it—let the composer write a suite called "The Hiawatha Suite"—then go back and start working from the composer's musical score.

On December 8, 1948, the studio held a showing for all of the artwork and story that had been done on the feature. While most praised the artwork, others feared that the approach was too "highbrow" in its seriousness, much like the earlier unsuccessful *Fantasia* (1940) and not what the audience would expect of a Disney animated feature.

Certainly the film faced many challenges including finding enough skilled animators who could handle drawing realistic human figures. It was also considered risky because the Disney Studio still had not recovered financially from World War II so the decision was made to concentrate on *Cinderella* (1950) which was a wise choice since it was both a critical and financial hit.

In September 1949, the story of Hiawatha was once again reworked so that it was told in flashback format to a white missionary to the tribe. In that way, it didn't have to be a straight story but focused on the best segments. Kelsey did even more storyboards. The villain Tadodaho disappeared and was replaced by the evil magician Pearl-Feather and he battled with Hiawatha for the big climax.

Most people feel that Walt abandoned the project by the end of 1949 but press articles about the forthcoming feature appeared as late as 1951.

At the same time Monogram Pictures cancelled a live action feature film about Hiawatha because of pressure at the time from the House on UnAmerican Activities committee who felt that Hiawatha's fame as "Great Peacemaker" might become a potential platform for communist propaganda because of the pacifist message.

Surely Walt who was keenly aware of what other studios were doing must have heard about all of this and as a staunch foe of communism wouldn't have wanted anything to do with something that might even inadvertently give aid to communists.

Abandoned Mickey Mouse Cartoons (1951)

The reason for so many unmade Mickey Mouse shorts was not just that a story idea didn't seem to gel but that Mickey was the victim of his own early success.

When interviewed in a 1949 issue of *Collier's* magazine, Walt stated:

> Mickey's decline was due to his heroic nature. He grew into such a legend that we couldn't gag around with him. He acquired as many taboos as a Western hero—no smoking, no drinking, no violence.

In a 1978 interview, Jack Hannah, who worked as a Disney storyman, told me:

> [Donald Duck's] temper made him an easier character to work with than Mickey Mouse. I remember many stories were started with Mickey but as soon as they started to rough the Mouse up, somebody would come up and say, "Well, that's more of a Donald Duck story" so they'd turn around and make it a Donald Duck story.
>
> Mickey was a little more the hero type so it was a little bit harder to find material for him. Walt had a special love for Mickey and I don't think he wanted to see Mickey roughed up.

One classic example of a Mickey story being transformed into a Donald story is *Yukon Mickey,* an unproduced short from the 1930s that was partially storyboarded with Mickey Mouse and then completely re-boarded with Donald Duck. Neither version had enough humor to satisfy Walt so it was abandoned.

In a story meeting on February 21, 1938, Walt talked about transforming the Mouse story into a Duck story:

> This picture might be suited better for the Duck as you would be able to use more personality with the Duck in spots where he would be laughing than you would with Mickey. The expression and the voice of the Duck would help it. It is a natural for the Duck to get in a situation like this—and the audience likes to see the Duck get it.

Jimmy MacDonald, who voiced Mickey for almost four decades, said:

Walt was very serious about the character. I remember when Walt was in a story meeting one time and they were showing him the storyboards and reading the dialogue. He was smiling and everybody thought, "Oh, this is great." If Walt was smiling, then it was going over well. But when he was through, he said, "No, we're not going to make it." And they couldn't understand why. Then he said, "I don't want Mickey put into those situations."

Sometimes a proposed Mickey story idea was just a simple sentence or two, like this one taken from a page of a dozen other quick ideas dating from the mid-1930s:

"Mickey is a poor farmer... Pete is a wealthy neighbor... Mickey finally triumphs over him in some way."

Sometimes there would be a short, written story outline or a selection of quickly done gag sketches to show the potential of an idea. Further development might reveal the story to be too flimsy, too labored, or just not appropriate for Mickey.

For instance, Mickey could only attack Pete if it was in defense of saving Minnie.

Here are just a few Mickey cartoons proposed in the 1930s that didn't get beyond the storyboard stage:

Navy Mickey: Mickey joins the Navy (just like Roy O. Disney did during World War I) and has run-ins with an admiral who is a bulldog.

Hillbilly Mickey: In the mountains, moonshiner Pete mistakes newcomer Mickey as a "revooner" sent to close down his still. Mickey would meet Minnie as a cute hillbilly girl at a dance.

Jungle Mickey: Mickey as a newsreel photographer in darkest Africa.

Pilgrim Mickey: This would have been the only Thanksgiving short ever made by the Disney Studio. There were several variations on the story, including Mickey recounting a tall tale to his nephews of how he went hunting for a turkey and ran into Indian trouble.

Tanglefoot: Taking place at a racetrack, Mickey is the owner of a horse with hay fever named Tanglefoot who appeared in Floyd Gottfredson's *Mickey Mouse* comic strip. According to Disney historian J.B. Kaufman, "Transcripts of the story meetings confirm that Walt Disney was intrigued with the project." At one story meeting, Walt warned: "Strive for the personality of the horse rather than relying on props for gags."

Pluto's Robot Twin: Mickey builds a robot dog to show Pluto how a good dog should behave. Unfortunately, the robot goes out of control and Pluto must rescue Mickey before the berserk automaton kills Mickey with its sharp teeth.

Mickey's Toothache: Because of an aching tooth, Mickey takes ether at the dentist and falls asleep. He dreams that Dentist Pete takes him to court (where a gigantic wisdom tooth is the judge) and charges Mickey with dental neglect. Mickey confronts creatures that are half-animal and half-dental instruments in a nightmarish world. Disney artists spent six months coming up with elaborate pencil drawings.

Prehistoric Mickey: The story of the first Mickey Mouse.

Mickey's Follies: Mickey, like the Great Flo Ziegfeld, is the host for a musical revue featuring all the standard Disney characters as well as some of the popular ones from the *Silly Symphony* series.

Mickey's Hotel: There were at least two versions of this story. One had Goofy and Donald as bumbling bellboys. Another had Mickey running his hotel with robots which, like all robots in animated cartoons, go out of control.

Many other story concepts are in the Disney vaults, including *The Time Machine,* where Mickey is sent back to the city of Atlantis and *Mickey's Sea Monster,* based on Walt's own suggestion of putting Mickey in a short version of Jules Verne's *20,000 Leagues Under the Sea.*

Some ideas did, however, progress almost to the final production stage. For example, two unreleased Mickey Mouse shorts from 1951 were over 90% completed, and many animation fans have urged Disney to either release these pencil tests or complete the animation.

One of them, *The Talking Dog,* focused more on Pluto than on Mickey, like many other Mickey shorts of the time.

Restoration specialist Scott MacQueen uncovered the scratch track (the preliminary rough voice and sound effects track) for *The Talking Dog* and some of its completed animation for use in his traveling 1997 presentation, *Disney's Unseen Treasures.*

MacQueen spent twelve years at the Disney company, beginning in 1991, where he oversaw the restoration and preservation of literally hundreds of classic cartoons as well as animated and live-action features.

The Mickey animation in *The Talking Dog* was done by legendary animator Fred Moore, known for his ability to bring the Mouse to life in a way that eluded so many others. The Pluto animation was done by another legendary animator Norm Ferguson, renowned for his earlier work on Pluto, like the scene of Pluto battling with flypaper. Milt Schaffer was the director of the short.

In the film, Pluto has been a bad dog messing up the house and a stern Mickey Mouse exiles him outside. As Pluto walks sadly along the side of the road, he is scooped up by a crooked con man (Pete) in a moving van lettered on its side with "Miracle Medicine Show."

Pete's concoction is "the medicine that takes warts off frogs, turns hiccups into teacups and guaranteed to cure the Texas tickle!" The tricky medicine man decides to entice customers to buy his wares by convincing them that Pluto can speak. Using his ventriloquism skills, he asks Pluto how he feels, and the poor pup seems to answer "Just like a piano... GRAND!"

Of course, to perform this "miracle", Pluto must first drink the horrible medicine, which makes him sick. Pluto soon gets tired of his sideshow career and longs to return home.

When Mickey can't find his beloved pet, he goes on a search that ends in a struggle with the medicine man on top of the careening truck as Pluto steers with his teeth. At one point, as they approach a covered bridge, Mickey and Pete leap from the top of the truck to the roof of the bridge and continue battling across it until they jump back on the truck as it exits the bridge on the other side. The driverless van soon smashes into a huge tree and Mickey recovers Pluto.

Mickey asks Pluto if he is "okay" and Pluto responds, "Grand!"

Disney producer Harry Tytle claimed that the short in its rough form got a low rating when it was screened for the other animators:

"I had thought *Talking Dog* was a weak story. Too much dialog and we didn't have the animators capable of doing a good job. At the time we first viewed the rough animation, I told Walt it was so bad that I called everyone concerned into a meeting. Three hundred feet of changes, new animation, went into the picture. The basic change was to make it a Pluto story but the animation by Ferguson was bad."

The Plight of the Bumblebee is the other nearly completed Mickey Mouse cartoon from 1951.

Once again, the primary Mickey Mouse animation was done by Fred Moore, with other scenes animated by Cliff Nordberg and Hal King. John Sibley may have been involved as well.

Director Jack Kinney offered his explanation why the short was abandoned before going to ink and paint:

> The best Mickey ever was never finished. It was called *The Plight of the Bumble Bee,* and it was all finished in animation. It had an awkward length, but Fred and Sib agreed that it could not be cut, so it was shelved.

Most animation scholars, however, agree that length was not the major factor in the cancellation of the film.

Also, *The Plight of the Bumble Bee* is not "the best Mickey ever", but it is a nice cartoon and a little out of the ordinary for Mickey. For one thing, he is dressed in a suit and a hat (think of Mickey dressed as Don Draper from the television series *Mad Men)* and calls to mind the "look" of Goofy as an office worker from cartoons of the same time period. It was a more suburban look that was common in that era's daily newspaper strips.

The film has straight voice-over narration. I asked voice expert Keith Scott whether he recognized the announcer's voice or any of the other voices in the film:

> I think the narrator could be Wendell Niles, Ken Niles' brother. The singer sounds a bit like the frog singer Bill Roberts in places, and the female sounds like Aileen Carlisle, but I am sure since the film was nearly completed that the Disney Archives could find the payment records from that time period to accurately identify the voices.

Walt always said that Mickey's voice, because of its limited range, could not sustain long stretches of dialog, so maybe that is the reason for the narration (just like in the typical suburban Goofy cartoons of the period, which were also directed by Kinney).

In the film, Mickey stumbles into a local bar, where he finds a bee named Hector singing "bebop" (a bee who is jazz bopping), but notices that the bee occasionally hits a beautiful operatic note. Mickey decides the bee is destined for bigger things, and becomes his manager by signing Hector to a contract. However, Mickey soon discovers that the reason Hector is singing in a bar is that he has a weakness for the nectar of flowers.

In fact, whenever he has a drink of nectar, he becomes a sloppy drunk. So, Mickey tries to keep Hector away from temptation. Unfortunately, for Hector's operatic debut, the stage set is decorated with flowers and Hector overindulges, sending the female opera diva on stage into a fit and a faint. Chaos ensues. After the performance, a defeated Mickey runs across a musical grasshopper outside and decides to try again.

The premise is similar to that of other animated cartoons, like *Dixieland Droopy* (MGM 1954), *One Froggy Evening* (Warners 1955), and *Finnegan's Flea* (Paramount 1958).

In 1981, Daan Jippes, who was working in the Consumer Productions division of the Disney Studio in Burbank, was browsing though some index cards in the Disney Archives when he found some information about Production 2428 (*The Plight of the Bumblebee*), including the location of three dusty boxes filled with stacks of animation, layouts, photographed storyboards, and x-sheets (exposure sheets). He also found the recorded soundtrack (with the final voices) on a transcription disc.

In an interview with Christopher Finch and Linda Rosenkrantz, Floyd Gottfredson, who did the *Mickey Mouse* comic strip for decades, pointed at some artwork on the wall above his drawing table and said:

This big model sheet up here was all made from drawings that [Fred Moore] made for... a featurette, called *The Plight of the Bumblebee*. Mickey had a bee that could buzz operatic numbers; he was a great virtuoso that way. But the bee had a weakness, he was a nectarholic: he'd get drunk on nectar, so Mickey had trouble controlling him this way. Fred got that picture about 90% animated, I understand, and Walt dumped it because he got scared of the alcoholic connotations.

The "alcoholic connotations" were probably not the reason the film was dropped because during this time period drunkenness was not considered a disease but rather a weakness and often was used as a springboard for comedic moments in films. In fact, at this same time, Walt was suggesting a cartoon based on drinking for the Goofy *How To* series. It was Roy O. Disney who stepped in and blocked production of that particular cartoon, according to producer Harry Tytle.

The Fred Moore model sheet was later used as the cover for a 1972 animator recruitment booklet from the Disney Studio entitled *What Do You Know About Disney?*

Under the supervision of animator and director Bunny Mattinson, and using all the elements that had been found, a picture reel of *The Plight of the Bumble Bee* was filmed and shown to Disney executives; unfortunately, Jeffrey Katzenberg (then Chairman of Walt Disney Studios) chose not to complete it.

After the screening, someone walked away with the picture reel—but fortunately, Mattinson had had the foresight to burn a one-quarter inch copy for himself. When Jippes was working on the television series *Mickey MouseWorks* in 1999, there was talk about finally finishing the short and using it on the series—but nothing came of it.

Perhaps the real reason for these two shorts being abandoned was Walt deciding that he couldn't generate a good enough story for the Mouse. He told an interviewer in 1951:

> I'm tired of Mickey now. For him, it's definitely trap time. The Mouse and I have been together for about 22 years. That's long enough for any association.

Those harsh words did not reflect Walt's true feelings, just his frustration at being unable to find a good vehicle for Mickey.

About the Author

Jim Korkis is an internationally respected Disney historian who has written hundreds of articles and two dozen books about all things Disney over the last forty years. Jim grew up in Glendale, California, where he was able to meet and interview Walt's original team of animators and Imagineers.

In 1995, he relocated to Orlando, Florida where he worked for Walt Disney World for fifteen years in a variety of capacities including Entertainment, Animation, Disney Institute, Disney University, College and International Programs, Disney Cruise Line, Disney Design Group, Disney Vacation Club, Yellow Shoes Marketing and more.

In those different roles, Jim had access to the multiple different departmental libraries on property as well as direct interaction with many of the people who worked on things that Disney never made from the Alpine Hotel for WDW near Blizzard Beach to the Fantasia Gardens attraction planned for the Magic Kingdom to the elaborate water show with a score written by Andrew Lloyd Webber announced for Crescent Lake entitled *Noah's Ark* among other things.

Jim's original research on Disney history has been used often by the Disney Company as well as other organizations including the Disney Family Museum.

Several websites currently frequently feature Jim's articles about Disney history:

- MousePlanet.com
- AllEars.net
- Yesterland.com
- CartoonResearch.com
- YourFirstVisit.net

In addition, Jim is a frequent guest on multiple podcasts as well as a consultant and keynote speaker to various businesses, schools and groups.

Jim is not currently an employee of the Disney Company.

To read more stories by Jim Korkis about Disney history, please check out his other books, all available from Theme Park Press:

- *Secret Stories of Extinct Disneyland (2019)*
- *The Unofficial Walt Disney World 1971 Companion (2019)*
- *The Vault of Walt: Volume 7, Christmas Edition* (2018)
- *Secret Stories of Mickey Mouse* (2018)
- *More Secret Stories of Disneyland* (2018)
- *Extra Secret Stories of Walt Disney World* (2018)
- *Call Me Walt* (2017)
- *Walt's Words* (2017)
- *Other Secret Stories of Walt Disney World* (2017)
- *Secret Stories of Disneyland* (2017)
- *The Vault of Walt: Volume 6* (2017)
- *Gremlin Trouble* (2017)
- *Donald Duck's Daddy* (2017)
- *More Secret Stories of Walt Disney World* (2016)
- *The Vault of Walt: Volume 5* (2016)
- *The Unofficial Disneyland 1955 Companion* (2016)
- *How to Be a Disney Historian* (2016)
- *Secret Stories of Walt Disney World* (2015)
- *The Vault of Walt: Volume 4* (2015)
- *Everything I Know I Learned from Disney Animated Features* (2015)
- *The Vault of Walt: Volume 3* (2014)
- *Animation Anecdotes* (2014)
- *Who's the Leader of the Club? Walt Disney's Leadership Lessons* (2014)
- *The Book of Mouse* (2013)
- *The Vault of Walt: Volume 2* (2013)
- *Who's Afraid of the Song of the South?* (2012)
- *The Revised Vault of Walt* (2012)

About Theme Park Press

Theme Park Press publishes books primarily about the Disney company, its history, culture, films, animation, and theme parks, as well as theme parks in general.

Our authors include noted historians, animators, Imagineers, and experts in the theme park industry.

We also publish many books by first-time authors, with topics ranging from fiction to theme park guides.

And we're always looking for new talent. If you'd like to write for us, or if you're interested in the many other titles in our catalog, please visit:

www.ThemeParkPress.com

. . . .

Theme Park Press Newsletter

Subscribe to our free email newsletter and enjoy:

- Free book downloads and giveaways
- Access to excerpts from our many books
- Announcements of forthcoming releases
- Exclusive additional content and chapters
- And more good stuff available nowhere else

To subscribe, visit www.ThemeParkPress.com, or send email to newsletter@themeparkpress.com.

Read more about these books
and our many other titles at:

www.ThemeParkPress.com